C000085172

ISBN 978-0-331-07437-6
PIBN 11011024

This book is a reproduction of an important historical work. Forgotten Books uses
state-of-the-art technology to digitally reconstruct the work, preserving the original format
whilst repairing imperfections present in the aged copy. In rare cases, an imperfection in
the original, such as a blemish or missing page, may be replicated in our edition. We do,
however, repair the vast majority of imperfections successfully; any imperfections that
remain are intentionally left to preserve the state of such historical works.

COPYRIGHTED

Vera Olmstead

Velma Carson

PRINTED AND BOUND BY
THE HUGH STEPHENS PRINTING CO.
JEFFERSON CITY, MO.

ENGRAVED BY
BURGER ENGRAVING COMPANY
KANSAS CITY, MO.

The ROYAL PURPLE 1 9 1 9

FOREWORD

DEDICATED to those Kansas State Agricultural College men who gave their lives on the battle field, Volume XI of the ROYAL PURPLE stands at the time as a monument to all Kansas Aggie spirit and devotion. Kansas Aggies won immortal glory for themselves, their Alma Mater and their country on the fields of France. Not a few were called upon to give the last full measure of devotion, and their names are forever written on our hearts.

While these men fought the good fight overseas, Alma Mater waged a successful battle against disrupting influences at home. The young women—and the few young men here to co-operate with them—who published this annual, are typical of the students who "carried on" in spite of continued interruptions and unprecedented conditions. Those who withstood difficulties and completed successfully a year of college work, demonstrated their persistent serious purpose, and their unquestionable fitness to survive.

The Kansas State Agricultural College faces a bright future. Another year will see many of the men of the service back in college class rooms, working with old-time vigor in preparation for peace-pursuits. Everywhere will be happy evidence of a return to normal conditions. The opportunities for our graduates of professional and technical training will be greatly enlarged as a result both of the active participation of the institution in war work and of the records made by Aggie men and women.

K. S. A. C. will continue to do effective work. It will open its doors wide to every class of the state's citizenship. Not for the few, but for the many, shall be the watchword, and we shall strive to make only the boundaries of the state the boundaries of our campus.

W. M. JARDINE.

THE 1919
ROYAL PURPLE

Published By The
SENIOR CLASS
Kansas State
Agricultural College

DEDICATION

To the 1919 Men
Who sleep in
    Flanders Fields,
We dedicate this
Class Book.
Humbly, Reverently
Thoughtfully.

ORDER OF BOOKS

64383

Is this the Royal Road to Learning?

"Where the Race of Men go by"

"Listen, from the Rock Walls Yonder, Comes the Sound of Fight and Fray"

"Where Genius Keeps His Vigils"

"The World was Well Made First, but Science Made it Better"

"*Wherein Our Women Folks are Taught the Mysteries of House and Home*"

*"How Many from Life's Desert Track have Strayed
Beneath this Well Remembered Shade"*

Student Army Training Corps Barracks

In Memoriam

Were you afraid to die
Our brothers, who went out into the night to find the morning?
We have not said good-bye—
To you, O splendid souls, we offer humble greeting.
The precious lives you give,
And give as freely as once you gave your voices chanting Jay Rah
Earns you the right to live
Forever, at liberty.   We are enslaved by an eternal debt.

They Gave Their Lives

Private Henry C. Altman, died at Fort Logan, Colorado, April 11, 1918.

Corporal Emory Ellsworth Baird, died of wounds, Bois Belleaux, June 22, 1918.

Private Joseph Parker Ball, killed in action, France, November 1, 1918.

Farrier Ralph V. Baker, died of disease, Base Hospital No. 45, France, October 4, 1918.

Sergeant Walter M. Blackledge, killed in action, Battle of the Argonne, September 26, 1918.

Private Walter Otto Brueckmann, died at Fort Riley, Kansas, October 13, 1918.

Private Macarthur B. Brush, died at Fort Riley, Kansas, March 15, 1918.

Lieutenant G. A. Cunningham, died at Detroit, Michigan, October 20, 1918.

Captain Willis E. Comfort, killed in action, Second Battle of Marne, July 18, 1918.

Private Glenn W. Davis, died at Camp Polk, North Carolina, November 30, 1918.

Private George R. Giles, killed in action, Battle of the Marne, July 21, 1918.

Lieutenant Ray Franklin Glover, died from accident, Langley Field, Virginia, October 14, 1918.

Private Roy F. Glover, died at Portland, Oregon, November 16, 1918.

Sergeant Lester D. Hamil, killed in action, St. Mihiel Drive, September 12, 1918.

Sergeant George Arthur Hopp, killed in action, Chateau-Thierry, June 13, 1918.

Private Calvin Lafayette Irwin, died from accident, Honolula, Hawaii, December 8, 1917.

Lieutenant Clede R. Keller, killed in action, Battle of the Argonne, September 28, 1918.

Sergeant Wilbur F. Lane, died from accident, Camp Dodge, Iowa, April 14, 1918.

Corporal Carl Lasswell, died of disease, Base Hospital No. 66, Neufchateau, October 9, 1918.

Private Walter McKinney, died at Camp Devens, Massachusetts, October 6, 1918.

Seaman Delbert Thomas Pollock, died at Naval Station, Seattle, Washington, October 28, 1918.

Lieutenant Cedric Hadaway Shaw, killed in action, St. Mihiel Drive, September 12, 1918.

Lieutenant John Slade, died at Camp Hunt, September 17, 1918.

Private Fred Taylor, died at Fort Riley, Kansas, October 12, 1918.

Lieutenant Loyd B. Vorhies, died from accident, Issondum, Indre, France, July 11, 1918.

Lieutenant Edward David Wells, killed in action, St. Mihiel Drive, September 12, 1918.

Private George Lee Wingate, killed in action, France, July 15, 1918.

JOHN SLADE

EDWARD D. WELLS

RAY F. GLOVER

DELBERT T. POLLOCK

LOYD B. VORHIES

CLEDE R. KELLER

JOSEPH P. BALL

LESTER D. HAMIL

GEORGE L. WINGATE

WALTER M. BLACKLEDGE

64383

G. A. Cunningham   MacArthur B. Brush

Willis E. Comfort

Carl Lasswell   Walter O. Brueckmann

FRED TAYLOR

C. LAFAYETTE IRWIN

CEDRIC SHAW

EMORY E. BAIRD

WILBUR F. LANE

WALTER McKINNEY

HENRY C. ALTMAN

GEORGE A. HOPP

GLENN W. DAVIS

RALPH V. BAKER

Honor Roll

Colonel E. C. Abbott, '93
Earl G. Abbott
Leon Abele
Harold Q. Abell
Wendell E. Abell
Lieutenant J. J. Abernethy, '16
A. A. Adams, '12
Sergeant D. A. Adams
Lieutenant-Colonel Emory S. Adams, '98
Lieutenant Franklin A. Adams, '09
Lieutenant Raymond V. Adams, '16
Edwin Osborne Adee
Mechanic J. F. Adee
Lieutenant M. E. Agnew
Corporal William Agnew
Marion Aiman
G. W. Ainlay
Sergeant W. G. Alderman, '13
George Alexander
Harry Whitford Alexander
Lynn E. Alexander
Sergeant Glenn Allen
Paul Allen
Lieutenant Leland Allis
C. N. Allison, '01
H. A. Allison
Mark Almgren
*Henry C. Altman
A. A. Anderson, '14
Bernard M. Anderson
Sergeant George E. Anderson
Sergeant George H. Anderson, '15
L. W. Anderson, '14
N. W. Anderson
Lieutenant Ray Anderson, '11
John W. Andrews
James Bell Angle
G. H. Ansdell, '16
Sergeant Alfred Apitz, '16
Willard Armstrong
A. C. Arnold, '17
Lieutenant George M. Arnold, '16
Theodore Arnold
Sergeant W. A. Atchison
Lieutenant C. E. Aubel
James Malcolm Aye, '18
Corporal John Ayers
E. M. Bachelor, '13
Harold Winthrop Bachelor
*Emory Ellsworth Baird
Sergeant H. E. Baird, '16
H. N. Baker
Lieutenant Paul K. Baker, '17
Ralph Baker, '16
*Ralph V. Baker
Stanley Baker, '16
Herbert Bales
*Joseph P. Ball
Russell Kenneth Ballou
Corporal Edgar Barger
Lieutenant Turner Barger
W. J. Barker
F. C. Borley
Glen B. Barley
Charles W. Barnes
Lieutenant J. B. Barnes, '17
John O. Barnes, '14
Sergeant Philip Barnes
Sergeant Samuel Barnes, '18
Sergeant Oliver Barnhart
B. L. Barofsky, '12
Lieutenant Carroll M. Barringer
Lieutenant T. R. Bartlett, '12
Harold Batchelor
M. E. Batchelor, '13
Sergeant Harold H. Bates
Lieutenant V. E. Bates
Frederick H. Bayer
Lieutenant Henry B. Bayer, '16
Theodore L. Bayer
B. B. Bayles

Pearl Beamen, '13
Corporal Merl Eldon Beard
Homer Glen Beaty
Lieutenant W. L. Beauchamp, '13
Ernest Bebb
Claude O. Beckett
Ralph Bell
Lieutenant James M. Belwood
Captain John R. Bender
Lieutenant-Colonel Louis B. Bender, '04
Ernest Benne
Walter Bergen
Lieutenant Frank Bergier, '14
Lieutenant A. C. Berry, '16
Lieutenant James Beverly
Lieutenant James H. Biddison
Trafford Bigger
Corporal Dean R. Billings
Corporal Everett Billings
J. A. Billings, '13
J. R. Bily
Raymond W. Binford
Sergeant John Bixby
Captain L. Harold Bixby
Lieutenant C. D. Blachly, '02
Corporal James J. Black
*Sergeant Walter Blackledge
Milton C. Blackman
Lieutenant Stewart Blackman
Lieutenant Frank S. Blair, '13
C. H. Blake, '13
Corporal William S. Blakley
Captain G. R. Blain
Frank Blecha, '18
Lieutenant O. F. Blecha
Robert E. Bock
Ed. Bogh
Lieutenant-Colonel C. H. Boice
Edward A. Bond
Corporal Henry Bondurant
Charles Bonnett
Lieutenant J. M. Boring
W. H. Borland
Charles Washington Bower
Lieutenant Cecil Bower
Gunner's Mate Sylvan Bower
Sergeant-Major Arthur W. Boyer
F. W. Boyd
Ensign J. I. Brady, '18
Lieutenant A. A. Brecheisen, '17
Lieutenant Carl S. Breese, '12
Roy Shipman Breese
George H. Brett, Jr.
Sergeant Arthur Brewer
Lieutenant Bruce B. Brewer
Lieutenant C. A. Brewer
C. T. Brewer
Cleve S. Briggs
Lieutenant R. A. Bright
Lieutenant Thornton F. Bright, '18
Sergeant Wellington T. Brink, '16
Harrison Broberg, '14
Lieutenant Oliver Broberg
J. B. Broddle
Lieutenant William H. Brooks
Sergeant Duke Brown
L. E. Brown
Lawrence E. Brown
Arthur Browne
Clarence Leland Browning
Lieutenant W. G. Bruce, '17
Paul Bruner
Martin Bruner
George Brusch
*MacArthur B. Brush, '16
Lieutenant W. A. Buck, '13
Captain W. V. Buck, '11
Major W. W. Buckley
Corporal V. E. Bundy
Holman L. Bunger
Major-General W. P. Burnham
George W. Burch
Lieutenant C. J. Burson, '01

Bryan W. Bushong
Corporal Henry Bushong
E. B. Butzerin
Albert C. Bux
Lieutenant B. F. Buzard, '12
Henry Byer
Francis C. Caldwell
Loys H. Caldwell
Major L. W. Call, '83
C. D. Calogeris, '16
Lieutenant J. W. Calvin, '06
Charles Campbell
John Lewis Campbell
Lieutenant Raymond Campbell
Lieutenant William Campbell
Milo G. Carey, '19
Sergeant Frank Carlson
Lieutenant John Carnahan, '17
Paul Carnahan
Roy E. Carr
Earl T. Carroll
Robert O. Carson
Raymond Carleton
J. O. Carter
Lou R. Carter
Glen M. Case
Sergeant William H. Case
Sergeant Floyd Casement
Edward H. Cass
W. N. Caton
Captain Russell R. Cave
Captain Wayne Bea Cave, '08
Colonel H. G. Cavenaugh
Colonel William A. Cavenaugh, '96
Lieutenant K. P. Cecil
Joseph E. Chaffee
Ray Chambers
Lieutenant Lawrence Champ
Lieutenant Charles K. Champlin
Edwin R. Chandler
Frank Chandler
Clarence B. Chapman
Harold Chapman
Lieutenant W. K. Charles
Roedel Childe
Corporal James Christner
Lieutenant Charles D. Christop
Charles Church
Theodore Citizen
Major E. L. Claeren
Clement G. Clarke, '88
D. C. Clark, '12
John A. Clarke
Thomas E. Clarke, '10
R. E. Cleland
A. R. Gless
Walter J. Coates
Lewis Cobb
Sergeant Luther Coblentz, '12
Captain Clay E. Coburn, '91
Major-General Frank Winston Coe
Harry Kirk Coe
Lloyd Cochran
E. B. Coffman
John P. Colburn
K. I. Coldwell
E. H. Coles
Chaplain Myron S. Collins
Ralph E. Collins
Arthur B. Collom
Harold B. Combs
George A. Comfort
Corporal Howard Comfort
*Captain W. E. Comfort, '14
Hobart Commack
Sergeant Aubrey Conrow, '18
John Warren Conrow
Lieutenant M. W. Converse, '18
Corporal Loyd L. Conwell, '13
Sergeant Arthur Cook
Jesse Alford Cook
Summer E. Copple
Henry Cornell

*Deceased

Captain J. H. Corsant. '13
Sergeant DeWitt Croft
Lieutenant Roy Crans
V. S. Crippen
Rex M. Criswell
Carl Crites
Homer Cross
Samuel H. Crotinger, '14
Miles Crouse
Oscar Cullen
Verne Culver
*Lieutenant George Andrew Cun-
  ningham, '17
S. W. Cunningham, '08
Ralph Curry, '21
C. E. Curtis
Sergeant R. E. Curtis, '16
William Curtis
Lieutenant Jay H. Cushman, '17
Lieutenant Robert Cushman
Sergeant W. D. Cusic, '14
Lieutenant Ernest E. Dale
F. L. Dale
N. E. Dale, '18
Marion Danby
D. Davidson
Lieutenant John F. Davidson, '13
Price J. Davies
Allan K. Davis
First Class Musician Charles A.
  Davis. '13
*Glenn W. Davis
Lieutenant N. H. Davis, '16
Paul B. Davis
Percy G. Davis, '11
Russell G. Davis
W. S. Davison, '10
Corporal Hubert A. Dawson
James R. Dawson, '17
Lieutenant George H. Dean. '16
Lieutenant Harlan Deaver, '10
Arthur Denman
Sergeant George E. Denman, '16
Rowland Dennen
Wilford Dennis
C. E. Depue
Corporal D. E. Dewey
Fabian C. Dickenson
W. E. Dickerson. '19
Sergeant Lawrence M. Dike
H. H. Dinsmore
Chief Carpenter's Mate Lyman
  LeRoy Dixon
Corporal Fred Dodge
Victor Dolecek
Granville Dorman
Lieutenant Ernest D. Doryland, '14
G. S. Douglass, '16
F. E. Dowling, '17
V. L. Drumm
Ensign J. E. DuBois, '18
Captain Hugh B. Dudley
K. R. Dudley
N. M. Dunbar
Lieutenant H. L. Dunham
Guy Earl
F. L. Early
Corporal Ray Eck
Colonel William H. Edelblute, '92
Colonel Glen E. Edgerton, '04
H. K. Ellinwood
Sergeant J. B. Elliot
Sergeant Leo Flliot
Roscoe V. Elliot
F. C. Ellis. '12
John F. Ellis
Sergeant Robert W. Ellis, '11
Fred Emerson
Master Signal Electrician J. G.
  Emerson
E. T. Englesby
Lieutenant C. R. Enlow
R. C. Erskine. '16
William R. Essick '18

Corporal James Estalock
Sergeant Morris Evans
Lieutenant H. C. Ewers, '15
L. H. Fairchild, '16
Ensign Hobart Fairman
Sibert Fairman
Jesse G. Falkenstein
Lieutenant S. S. Fay, '05
Corporal H. H. Fayman
Lieutenant H. M. Fayman
Captain Shelby G. Fell, '15
C. I. Felps, '12
Malcolm Fergus
A. M. Ferguson
John Ferguson
*Ralph Ferguson
Ray Ferree
George Ferrier
W. W. Fetro
Paul L. Fetzer
Lieutenant Clarence A. Fickel
Floyd Fike
Lieutenant P. L. Findley
Corporal Homer Fink
Charles E. Finney
Earl F. Fishel
Sergeant George W. Fisher
H. C. Fisher
G. W. Fisher
Sergeant Otto F. Fisher
Lieutenant G. W. FitzGerald. '16
Lieutenant Irl F. Fleming. '17
A. F. Fletcher
Sergeant Floyd Fletcher
Lieutenant J. H. Flora, '17
Glick Fockele, '02
D. F. Foote, '09
Asa Ford
Corporal K. L. Ford
A. W. Foster
Ralph L. Foster
Captain I. L. Fowler. '15
Frank E. Fox
Major Philip Fox. '97
Edward R. Frank, '18
Lieutenant Harve Frank
Ensign Charles Anthony Franken-
  hoff, '18
Ralph Franklin
George Adam Franz
Sergeant Herbert A. Frazier
Sergeant John Fredenburg
Carl Freed
James Freeland
I. G. Freeman, '17
Herbert Freese
F. H. Freeto, '15
H. H. Frizell, '16
Lieutenant Dewey Fullington
Ralph Fulton
W. P. Gaiser, '18
O. D. Gardner
Samuel Ray Gardner
T. O. Garinger
Lieutenant J. L. Garlough. '16
C. W. Gartrell, '15
Lieutenant L. E. Gaston
Captain W. S. Gearhart
D. N. Geeslin
Henry O. Gemar
Allen George
Clarence R. George
Captain Jesse George, '07
Lieutenant R. W. Getty, '12
Lieutenant L. C. Geisendorf, '15
Lester E. Gfeller
*George R. Giles
G. S. Gillespie, '13
Lieutenant H. M. Gillespie
Lieutenant Walter Gillespie
C. L. Gilruth
B. H. Gilmore, '13
F. E. Gilmore, '16
Captain H. B. Gilstrap, '91

Sergeant Howard Gingery
Lieutenant John C. Gist, '14
George W. Givens
B. E. Gleason
*Lieutenant Ray F. Glover
Lieutenant C. S. Goldsmith. '14
W. H. Goldsmith, '11
Willis Goldsmith
Robert Goodwin
Wilbur Ross Gore, '17
Archie R. Graham
Captain Ardi M. Graham
Lieutenant Frank H. Graham
Captain Alfred A. Grant
Earl I. Graul
Charles Gregory
Lieutenant D. M. Green, '17
Lieutenant-Colonel Ned M. Green,
  '97
L. P. Greenbank
Lieutenant B. F. Griffin. '18
P. F. Griffin
Lewellen Griffing
Corporal Roy E. Griffiths
L. G. Gross, '15
S. S. Gross, '10
Sergeant L. E. Grube. '13
Luke A. Guilfoyle
F. H. Gulick
Sergeant John Gulledge
Corporal Edwin Gunn
Harry Gunning, '16
Lieutenant George F. Haas, '14
Roy William Haege
L. V. Haegert, '16
Lieutenant J. S. Hagan. '16
Lieutenant W. S. Hagan
Lieutenant W. W. Haggard, '15
L. R. Hain, '11
Sergeant Cecil W. Haines. '14
Lieutenant Charles Haines, '09
Captain C. T. Halbert, '16
F. L. Hall
John R. Hall, Jr.
Ray Everett Hall
*Lester Hamil
George Hamilton
Glen Hamilton
Gordon W. Hamilton
Lloyd B. Hamilton
Lawrence Hammond
A. C. Hancock, '18
Lieutenant Gaylord Hancock
Corporal Floyd Hanna
Lawton M. Hanna
R. J. Hanna
Sergeant Frank K. Hansen
Lieutenant Anton Hanson, '09
Lieutenant Gustaf W. Hanson, '00
Captain Harry W. Hanson
Major-General James G. Harbord
  '86
Loyal G. Harris
Lieutenant R. I. Harris, '12
Tom Harris, '14
Corporal Jesse E. Harrold
Earl R. Harrouff. '16
Budford Hartman
Ernest Hartman
Fred G. Hartwig, '16
Lieutenant M. E. Hartzler, '14
Andrew M. Harvey
H. S. Harvey
Nathan D. Harwood
Frank Haucke
Edward Haug
Charles M. Haughton
Corporal Floyd Hawkins
Carl Hawkinson
A. L. Haydar
Captain A. L. Hazen
Edwin Chapin Headley
George M. Hedges

*Deceased.

George G. Hedrick
H. B. Hedrick
Lieutenant H. R. Heim, '06
Major-General E. A. Helmick
Joseph E. Helt
C. R. Hemphill
Lieutenant Homer Henney
H. J. Henny
E. A. Hepler
Walter A. Hepler, '14
Corporal Ralph H. Heppe
Ethan Allen Herr
W. K. Hervey, '16
Corporal Grant W. Herzog
Sergeant C. W. Hestwood, '18
Lieutenant George Hewey
Lieutenant Lyman R. Hiatt, '17
C. W. Hickok, '16
Francis M. Hill
Jack Hill
Philip G. Hill
Lieutenant-Colonel Roy E. Hill
T. Newton Hill, '09
Russell D. Hilliard
Glenn F. Hicks
Ross Hicks
Verny O. High
Sergeant R. Reginold Hinde
O. A. Hindman
Jackson Benjamin Hinds
Orin W. Hinshaw
Fred W. Hiss
Corporal Theodore Hobble
Lieutenant L. S. Hobbs
Herman G. Hockman
Archie Loy Hodgson, '14
Lieutenant A. G. Hogan
Charles T. Holbert
Abraham Holderman
Lieutenant Harold Hollister
S. W. Honeywell
Captain Robert Hood
Sergeant C. A. Hooker, '15
D. R. Hooten
Harold W. Hoots
Ercile Hoke
Merton Hoke
Paul Holmes
Harry Hope
Lieutenant A. E. Hopkins, '16
*Sergeant G. Arthur Hopp, '17
G. A. Hopp, '15
Dick Hopper
Lieutenant Henry R. Horak, '16
P. W. Houston
Walter C. Howard, '77
Sergeant C. B. Howe
Charles W. Howe
Lieutenant Frank R. Howe, '14
Willis W. Hubbard
O. L. Hubp, '15
Lieutenant Donald Hudson
James Huey
Eugene Huff
Carl F. Huffman, '17
Lieutenant D. D. Hughes
Captain James C. Hughes
C. D. Hultgren, '17
Corporal Elmer C. Humphrey
Lieutenant Edwin H. Hungerford, '12
*Lieutenant Harry F. Hunt, '13
Lieutenant Jay Hunt
Lieutenant O. W. Hunter, '09
C. C. Key, '18
Clyde Cecil Key
Lieutenant John Kiene, '16
Corporal Robert Kilbourne
Master Electrician Robert Kimble
Lieutenant S. R. Kimble
Clare Kimport
G. B. Kimport
J. Carroll King
Lieutenant Paul R. King, '15

Captain Keith E. Kinyon, '17
Henry J. Kilwer
Lieutenant R. F. Kirshner
R. V. Knapp
Clark C. Kniseley
William Knostman
T. R. Knowles
Raymond S. Knox
George Kolterman, '13
Frank Kramer, '14
Ralph Kratz
Les Lair, '11
D. G. Lake
Lieutenant Clarence Lambert, '07
Corporal Ira K. Landon
*Sergeant Wilbur Lane
Ralph Lapsley
*Carl F. Lasswell
A. E. Lawson, '16
E. C. Lee
Lieutenant J. M. Lee
Paul Lemly
*Lieutenant C. L. Lewis
Frank C. Lewis, '13
Lieutenant R. B. Leydig, '17
Carleton Glen Libby
Captain Joe G. Lill, '09 and '11
John Lill
E. C. Lindholm
F. M. Lindsay
M. A. Lindsay, '16
Captain H. D. Linscott, '16
James R. Little
J. R. Little, '15
Captain George M. Logan, '02
Lieutenant Carl Long, '08
Lieutenant Charles E. Long
Clyde Long
Corporal J. P. Loomis, '16
W. J. Loomis, '15
Ray Losh
R. O. Lowrance
Lieutenant Bruce Lovett
W. E. Lovett
Lieutenant O. M. Low
Walter M. Lowry
Lieutenant Ralph Lucier
Jay Lush, '17
Gerard Lyle
Lieutenant Samuel P. Lyle
J. M. Lyons, '13
J. S. McBride, '14
Lieutenant Fay E. McCall, '13
R. W. McCall
J. Donald McCallum, '14
Lieutenant G. E. McCarthy
Carl G. McCaslin
Howard S. McClanahan
Robert McClanahan, '16
Captain Harold McClelland, '16
Robert U. McClenahan, '16
Captain W. A. McCullough, '98
Sergeant Elmer David McCollum
Corporal Samuel McCullough
Lieutenant J. H. McDonnall, '15
Lieutenant G. B. MacDonnell
Dan McElvain
Everett McGalliard
Captain R. E. McGarraugh, '17
W. A. McGinley
Dan J. McGinty
W. C. McGraw
Lieutenant R. Donald MacGregor
Sergeant Dilts McHugh
C. E. McIlrath
Lieutenant William McIllwain
E. L. McIntosh
Calvin McInturff
J. H. McKee
William A. McKinley
*Walter McKinney
A. J. Mack, '12
Harold Mackey
Aubrey MacLee

Captain Roscoe I. MacMillan
Claude McMillan
Hubert A. McNamee
G. W. McVey
Lieutenant Donald E. MacLeod, '18
Ivor Orin Mall
Captain Carl Mallon, '07
Albert J. Mengelsdorf, '16
Paul LeRoy Mann
Corporal Earle Manners
E. J. Manninger
Lieutenant George E. Manzer, '18
A. L. Marble, '15
Clair Marbley
Sergeant Otto I. Markham, '16
M. G. Markley
W. C. Marrs
Roy Edwin Mars
Lieutenant Schuyler Marshall
S. S. Marshall
Lieutenant E. R. Martin, '16
Earl W. Martin
Corporal William Luther Martin
J. R. Mason, '16
K. P. Mason, '04
L. M. Mason, '17
Rollo Mather
Major L. O. Mathews
Merritt Matthews
Clarence R. Mattison
Captain Walter E. Mathewson, '01
Captain Lewis A. Maury
R. W. May
Ray Means
Wilson C. Means
W. C. Meldrum, '14
Carl J. Merner
G. J. Mibeck
Chester Howard Middleton
Edgar C. Miller, '17
Ernest Miller
G. A. Miller
H. P. Miller
Lieutenant R. W. Miller
F. W. Milner, '15
Lieutenant Leo Mingenbeck
J. R. Mingle
Lieutenant S. M. Mitchell
J. D. Montague
Ben Moore
Thomas Edwin Moore, '16
Lieutenant W. D. Moore, '12
Lieutenant Riley E. Morgan
Sergeant Charles Morris
E. Morrison
Major General John H. Morrison
R. V. Morrison
W. S. Morrow
Corporal J. Clare Morton
Lieutenant Leo C. Moser
F. E. Moss, '13
H. G. Mosshart
Captain J. B. Mudge, '14
M. M. Muguerditchian
Sergeant Harry A. Muir
Royal M. Mullen
George Munsell
Lieutenant R. V. Murphy
R. A. Muttkowski
Corporal Lawrence M. Nabours, '15
Lieutenant Charles M. Neiman, '13
Chester Neiswender
Sergeant Raymond R. Neiswender, '16
Alfred Nelson, '17
H. H. Nelson
P. L. Netterville, '18
Francis Nettleton
Dewey Newcombe
Clell A. Newell
Sergeant Rav H. Newkirk
George Newman

*Deceased.

HONOR ROLL—Continued

Lieutenant Harold Newton
Corporal Raymond C. Nickols
Lieutenant Arthur Clough Nichols
Floyd B. Nichols, '12
Captain R. T. Nichols, '99
Brigadier-General W. J. Nicholson
Sergeant Charles Nitcher
Vernon Noble
Paul A. Noce
Lieutenant Edgar L. Noel, '16
Oscar Norby, '12
F. E. Nordeen
William Axtell Norman
O. E. Norton
D. F. Novak
Lieutenant W. A. Nye
Sergeant D. V. O'Harro
Charles O'Leary
Lieutenant C. E. O'Neal
H. O'Neil
Captain William P. J. O'Neill
Thomas O'Reilly
Floyd E. Oakes
Guy Oden
Lloyd V. Oglevie
Sergeant G. W. Oliver
Lieutenant-Colonel H. D. Orr, '99
Burton S. Orr, '07
William Orr
Henry Osoba
Claude B. Owen
Everett Oxley
Sergeant Burr H. Ozment
Lieutenant-Colonel O. G. Palmer, '87
Lieutenant H. O. Parker, '13
Captain L. R. Parkerson, '16
Sergeant Elroy Parnell
Lieutenant R. D. Parrish, '14
First Sergeant J. D. Parsons, '15
C. H. Pate
Lieutenant Amos O. Payne
Floyd Payne
Charles Francis Payton
Aaron E. Pearson, '14
John Thomas Pearson
Lieutenant Nevels Pearson
Lieutenant Arthur F. Peine
Allan Penine
Lieutenant E. Q. Perry, '15
Orin Ross Peterson
S. D. Petrie
William Pfaff
J. A. N. Plegar
Carroll Phillips
Lieutenant Roy Phillips, '14
Glen Phinney, '16
Sergeant Elmo Phipps
Gaylord L. Phipps
Robert B. Piatt
Lieutenant Floyd M. Pickrell
Paul Pieratt
Corporal William Dale Pierce
Lieutenant E. F. Pile, '16
Corporal Eli Paul Pinet
Perrie Pitts, '18
L. A. Plumb
Claude A. Poland
*Delbert T. Pollock
Lieutenant Rayburn Potter, '15
Corporal James E. Pratt
Martin Pressgrove
C. E. Prock
Ernest Henry Ptacek, '18
Leo Dewey Ptacek
Lieutenant D. M. Purdy, '17
Lieutenant J. V. Quigley, '16
Lieutenant Arthur W. Quinlan
John M. Quinn
Henry P. Quinn
K. S. Quisenberry
Harold Ragle
Roland C. Ragle
George H. Railsback, '14

Lieutenant Wayne Ramage, '16
C. Ramsey
Lieutenant Earl Ramsey, '16
Lieutenant Ralph P. Ramsey, '16
Alfred Kirk Ramy
Delmer W. Randall, '99
Corporal Ralph Randell
Lee William Randels
Sergeant William A. Rankin
Captain Hile Rannells, '10
Lieutenant Elliot Ranney, '16
Captain S. M. Ransopher, '11
George T. Ratliffe, '10
Captain F. R. Rawson, '16
Paul C. Rawson, '17
Earl H. Raymond
W. S. Read, '98
Sergeant W. S. Read
Lieutenant George T. Reaugh, '16
Lieutenant Zeno Rechel
C. J. Reed, '12
Marion Reed
Lieutenant O. W. Reed
Lyman J. Rees
J. D. Reeves
George Reisner
Lloyd M. Reudy, '16
Captain Guy C. ReXroad, '09
Lawrence Reyburn
George W. Rhine
Captain L. A. Richards, '15
Ralph Richards
Sergeant Dorian P. Ricord, '16
Major J. D. Riddell, '93
Lieutenant Glenn A. Riley
F. L. Rimbach
Hugh Rippey
Fred Robb
Sergeant-Major J. H. Robert
Lloyd W. Roberts
F. Lee Robinson
Corporal Lynn A. Robinson, '13
Sergeant Temple M. Robinson
W. H. Robinson, '16
Sergeant C. A. Roda
Sergeant Carl Otto Roda
Lieutenant C. J. Rodenwald
W. J. Rogers
R. E. Romig
E. W. Roney
Captain Frank Root, '14
David S. Rose
Corporal Harold E. Rose
Master Engineer Worth D. Ross, '11
Louis Ross
Scott Ross
C. R. Rothbrock
H. D. Rothbrock
Irvin T. Rothbrock
Sergeant Clifford S. Rude
Fred J. Ruffner
Elliott Rundquist
W. F. Runyen
Lieutenant Guy Russell
Homer Russell
Sergeant O. V. Russell
Michael Ryan, '07
O. O. St. John
Lieutenant Ralph St. John, '17
Arthur J. Sahlberg
Lieutenant Glenn C. Salisbury
J. B. Salisbury
Morse H. Salisbury
Kenneth A. Sanborn
Carrew Sanders
William E. Sanders
Lieutenant Elbridge Sanders, '13
George Sanford
Lieutenant Frank Sargent, '15
Robert Saxon
Captain Chauncey Sawyer
Corporal Glen Sawyer
Albert L. Schell, '09

Captain Robert Schmidt
F. Smith Schneider
George M. Schooler
Lieutenant George R. Schroll
Lieutenant Elmer Schultz
Lieutenant William A. Schuster, '13
Lieutenant Herschel Scott, M. S., '17
Lee Scott
Corporal Flavel Scriven
R. Maurice Sears
Captain R. A. Seaton, '04
R. J. Sedivy, '16
Clarence Seeber
Abel Segel, '12
Chester Selfridge
Corporal Palmer W. Selfridge
R. E. Sellers, '16
Lieutenant John Sellon, '17
Colonel Pearl M. Shaffer
Major E. L. Shattuck, '07
*Lieutenant Cedric H. Shaw
Lieutenant Leslie Shaw
Lieutenant Warren R. Sheff, '17
Lieutenant R. A. Shelly, '15
Lieutenant H. H. Sherrard, '14
Frank Sherill
Samuel Sherwood
George N. Shick, '16
Harry Kenneth Shideler
Balford Q. Shields, '18
Corporal Simon P. Shields, '18
W. H. Shinkle
Ira John Shoup
T. L. Shuart
Lieutenant Dave Shull, '16
Sergeant Frank Sidorfsky, '14
Captain C. M. Siever
Sergeant Clarence Sigler
Lieutenant W. E. Simonsen '12
Lieutenant Paul J. Simpson
Albert Sims
R. Sitterson
Captain Emmett W. Skinner, '16
Owen Skinner
Lieutenant W. N. Skourup, '15
*Lieutenant John Slade
Corporal Orla D. Small
A. E. Smith
Lieutenant Corwin C. Smith, '15
Lieutenant Erle Hazlett Smith, '15
E. L. Smith
Lieutenant George W. Smith, '93
Lieutenant Guy C. Smith, '16
Harry C. Smith
Lieutenant John Earl Smith
June B. Smith
Leslie F. Smith
O. E. Smith, '15
Captain Oliver R. Smith, '98
Sam A. Smith
U. J. Smith, '14
W. E. Smith
W. F. Smith, '15
W. R. Smith, '14
Harold Snell
Harold W. Snell, '17
Corporal C. W. Snodgrass
Lucien Snyder
J. L. Snyder
Lyman H. Sommer
Martin Soule
James Sparks
Sergeant Joe Speer
Lieutenant Arthur B. Sperry
Lieutenant Lewis Sponsler
Sergeant R. C. Spratt
Captain Elmer G. Stahl, '13
Dean R. Stanley
Ralph Stanley, '18
Lieutenant William Edward Stanley, '12
Sergeant Oscar Steanson
W. S. Stevens

*Deceased.

Everett Stewart
Arthur H. Stewe
Ross W. Stice
Lieutenant M. Stigers
Sergeant Joseph Stinson
J. D. Stoddard
Corporal Claude Stone
Forrest R. Stone
Lowell M. Stone
Lieutenant V. D. Stone, '13
Charles E. Strain, '13
R. E. Straka, '18
Sergeant Ray Allen Stratford
Lieutenant C. J. Stratton, '11
Corporal Jay W. Stratton, '16
Captain Alden G. Strong, '11
Lieutenant John Godfrey Stutz
Jerry P. Sullivan
Giles Sullivan
Lieutenant Harlan R. Sumner, '16
Percy W. Swain
Rollin Swaller
Arthur F. Swanson
Merton Swanson
Harry J. Swarm
Captain Joseph B. Sweet. '17
Harold J. Swingle
Leonhardt Swingle, '13
Ray S. Talley
Sergeant Leslie Tanner
D. C. Tate, '16
*Fred Taylor
George E. Taylor
George Emery Taylor
Glenn Taylor
Ira Earl Taylor, '13
*I. I. Taylor
Russell L. Taylor
W. F. Taylor
Corporal Earl H. Teagarden
Harvey D. Tebow
Ralph Terrill
Robert Terrill
George Tewell
Captain George I. Thatcher, '10
Lieutenant O. M. Thatcher
Lieutenant Owen Thackery
Lieutenant W. L. Thackery, '18
Lieutenant Harold A. Thackrey, '14
Lieutenant O. M. Thatcher
Lieutenant Donald Cheney Thayer
Lieutenant A. L. Theiss
Charles D. Thomas, '17
L. R. Thomas, '18
Lewis Thompson
Olis Thompson
Rudolph W. Thompson
Lieutenant Colonel Claude B.
Thummel, '05
Sergeant Graydon Tilbury, '15
Lieutenant John Tillotson
L. A. Tilton
Lewis Timmons
C. M. Tinkler
Corporal George Titus
Sergeant Earl Tobler
Sergeant George O. Tolman
Lieutenant Topping
Corporal Lester G. Tubbs, '17
Richard Tunstall
Lieutenant Floyd C. Turner
F. S. Turner, '17
Lieutenant Wright Turner
L. M. Umberger
Mark F. Upson
Captain Sidney Vandenburg, '16
B. Vandiver
Lieutenant R. D. Van Nordstrand,
'12
Ralph Van Trine
Lieutenant Harry Van Tuyl, '17

Cedric Van Vliet
John W. Van Vliet
Julius P. Van Vliet, '15
Lieutenant L. G. Van Zile
Lieutenent Ralph P. Van Zile, '16
Harold Hurt
Lieutenant L. E. Hutto, '13
Lieutenant A. E. Hylton, '16
Paul R. Inel
Lieutenant Carl L. Ipsen. '13
*Calvin L. Irwin
Fred Irwin
Lieutenant Paul Jackson, '15
James L. Jacobson. '15
Corporal Leslie E. Jacobson
Paul E. Jacobson
C. R. Jacobus, '09
Thomas James
Lieutenant William C. Janssen
H. F. Jenkins
C. D. Jennison
Edward Jilka
B. O. Johnson, '11
Lieutenant F. W. Johnson, '15
Marvin Johnson
Corporal Myron Johnson
Orla J. Johnson
Scott Johnson
C. O. Johnston, '18
A. E. Jones
Lieutenant Clarence Jones, '13
Lieutenant E. C. Jones, '16
Lieutenant Ralph C. Jones, '13
Lieutenant Francis N. Jordan
Russel Jump
Lieutenant Horace L. Kapka
Corporal Walter Karlowski
George A. Kauffman
Stephen Kauffman
G. W. Keith
Captain E. H. Kellogg. '11
Corporal Frank Kellog
Leslie C. Kees
Lieutenant Glenn Keith, '17
Lieutenant C. R. Keller
Floyd B. Kelly
Lieutenant George L. Kelly
Loren Kelsey
Myron Kelsey
Rex Kendall
Lieutenant Edward Kernohan, '14
Lieutenant R. Kerr, '17
Lieutenant Robert Kerr, Jr.
Lieutenant J. K. Kershner
Sergeant E. V. Kessinger, '17
Romney C. Ketterman. '15
Lieutenant Edgar A. Vaughn, '12
Lyman Ray Vawter
Sergeant W. F. Veatch
Lieutenant Ray Vermette
Carl M. Vermillion
Lieutenant T. K. Vincent. '16
*Lieutenant Lloyd Vorhees
John Ralph Voris
Sergeant D. H. Wageman
H. A. Wagner
Harold Wagoner
Lieutenant A. J. Walker
Captain H. B. Walker
Leon Wallace
Lieutenant Elsmere J. Walters, '13
Rees C. Warren
Lieutenant George Washburn
Lawrence Wassinger
M. C. Watkins
Captain F. A. Waugh, '91
Frederick V. Waugh
Carl Webb
J. Everett Weeks
R. J. Weinheimer
Corporal Claude Weir

*Lieutenant E. D. Wells
Lieutenant John Hanna Welsh, '16
Corporal Willard Welsh
F. B. Wenn
Sergeant Mark Wentz
Captain Edward N. Wentworth
W. C. Wessler
Lieutenant James West, '12
C. E. Wettig
Lieutenant Edwin Wheatly
Edwin Frederick Whedon
Lieutenant-Colonel Earl Wheeler,
'05
Colonel Mark Wheeler, '97
Captain C. E. Whipple
Frank Whipple
Wilbur Whitacre
John D. Whitcomb
Sergeant Jesse White
Lieutenant L. P. Whitehead. '16
Sergeant Gilbert Whitsett
A. C. Whittacre
Laurence W. Wiest
Rex A. Wilbur
Captain Marshall P. Wilder
H. L. Wilkins
Lieutenant H. W. Wilkinson, '11
Sergeant W. L. Willhoite, '16
J. D. Williams
Lieutenant J. M. Williams
J. W. Williams
Lieutenant Arleigh L. Willis
L. A. Wilsey
Albert E. Wilson
Albert W. Wilson
D. A. Wilson
Frew T. Wilson
Sergeant George W. Wilson
Lawrence Wilson
Lieutenant R T. Wilson
W. C. Wilson.
Sergeant W. Clyde Wilson
William D. Wilson
William M. Wilson
Paul Winchell
*George Lee Wingate
William R. Winget
Sergeant Jesse Wingfield
Brigadier-General Frank Winston
Harberd Wise
R. E. Wiseman
Sergeant Fred Widmoyer
James A. Williamson
Milton S. Winter
Corporal C. R. Witham, '18
H. P. Witham
Lieutenant C. C. Wolcott, '13
Raymond M. Wolfe
Corporal Earl Wood
Corporal Harry E. Wood
Howard B. Wood
Sergeant John C. Wood
Sergeant John Kirk Wood
John S. Wood, '16
Lawrence Woods
Sergeant-Major Shelby M. Woods
Lieutenant D. M. Wooley
David F. Wooster
Irving Wulfekuhler
J. R. Worthington
Lieutenant J. W. Worthington, '17
C. W. Wyland, '15
Lieutenant H. B. Yocum
Lieutenant Chauncey Yeoman
Lieutenant T. Yost
Corporal Fred F. Young
Sergeant Roy Young, '14
Oscar W. Youngberg
Harold M. Youngmeyer
Charles Zimmerman

---

*Deceased.

MAJOR-GENERAL JAMES G. HARBORD, '87

His Men Saved Paris

IN MAY, 1918, a German flood was sweeping down the Marne towards Paris. Divisions of resolute Frenchmen had made stand after stand, had thrown themselves unselfishly against their enemies, but the Hun armies rolled on. General Foch, dismayed, called on the Americans to save the French capital. General Pershing selected the Second Division.

After marching day and night, slopping through mud and braving summer heat, the Second arrived at Chateau-Thierry. A brigade immediately was thrown into line. The Americans struck hard and the invaders, surprised, were halted, reeled, and then gave way before a demon-like counter attack. A brigade of Americans had saved Paris, had given France new hope, had proved the mettle of American troops. These men France thanked were soldiers of the Fourth Brigade, U. S. Marines, commanded by an Aggie man, Brigadier-General James G. Harbord, '87· Following is an extract from a letter General Harbord wrote to his mother, Mrs. Effie Harbord of Manhattan on June 2, the second day of the drive:

"One of my regiments was put in line hurriedly yesterday afternoon. Today, part of another one. They have done splendidly today, and the slopes are piled with dead Germans in one place where the machine guns caught them· Everything seems to be going all right, and I don't think the Germans will offend much farther in this part of the line."

Later, on June 9, after the General and his brigade had been commended in orders from army headquarters—it was the first brigade to be so honored— General Harbord wrote:

"Naturally, I am feeling very happy and glad over it, though saddened by the thought of the brave men lost. Eleven officers of the brigade have been killed this week, many more wounded, and several hundreds of men killed and wounded. But the brigade has stood like a rock, and as the French papers said, 'Their gallantry put a brake on the German advance.'"

Although the most sensational deed of General Harbord, the repulse at Chateau-Thierry is only a small part of the work this Aggie man has been doing. First of all he went to France as Chief of Staff to General Pershing, and for more than a year was the executive officer of the Expeditionary Forces. The Marne battle won him promotion, and as Major-General he assumed command of the Second Division.

The tremendous amount of quartermaster work in France brought General Pershing new problems, and he called upon General Harbord to solve them. The Aggie man was made Chief of the Service of Supplies, a position second in importance to that of the Commanding General.

Men of '19 Who Served

L EADING all classes of the college in the number of men in service and in the roll of those who lost their lives, the Class of '19 has a service record of which every member is proud. Of the approximately eighteen hundred Aggie men who wore the khaki or the blue, nearly two hundred are known to have been members of this year's graduating class. The proportion of men who made the sacrifice is even greater, for eight of the twenty-nine who are known to have died would have received their degrees this spring.

In the list of the men of '19 who were lost is included the names of some of the most prominent students of the college. In the one year he competed in college athletics, "Eddie" Wells, who would have finished his course in February of this year, was accorded the position of fullback on the All-Missouri Valley football eleven and had been placed as a guard on the picked basket ball five of the conference. He was killed in action while advancing with his men of the Rainbow Division in the St. Mihiel drive, September 12, 1918. "Eddie" was a first lieutenant. In the same battle and on the same date, Sergeant Lester B. Hamil lost his life in action. For his bravery in the engagement, Sergeant Hamil was cited by his regimental commander. He was a member of the 353rd Infantry of the famous Eighty-ninth Division, which was trained by General Leonard Wood at Camp Funston, twelve miles from Manhattan.

Clede R. Keller, a former cadet officer, has been missing in action since September —, 1918, and friends practically have given up hopes for his return. Keller, who was a first lieutenant with Company "I," a Manhattan unit in the Thirty-fifth Division, is known to have been severely wounded in action. A number of men of his company have said that he was killed by the explosion of a shell while litter-bearers were carrying him to a dressing station. His name, however, has not appeared on war department lists.

Two aviators, Loyd Vorhies and Ray F. Glover, have been killed in airplane accidents. Both were officers. Vorhies, who was promising material for the Aggie track team, died when his machine fell in France, and Glover was killed in an accident at Langley Field, Virginia.

C. LaFayette Irwin died from injuries received in a football game. He was stationed at Honolula, Hawaii.

The '19 Service Record

Edwin O. Adee
Corporal William Agnew
Sergeant Glenn Allen
Lieutenant Leland Allis
Nelson J. Anderson
James B. Angle
Lieutenant Turner Barger
H. D. Barnes
Lieutenant Carrol M. Barringer
Arthur E. Bate
Fred Beaudette
Ernest Bebb
Lieutenant Welton W. Bell
Walter Bergen
T. W. Bigger
Corporal James J. Black
George Y. Blair
William S. Blakely
Lieutenant Cecil Bower
Lieutenant Bruce B. Brewer
Lieutenant Oliver Broberg
Sergeant Duke Brown
Sergeant Frank Carlson
Joseph Cassidy
Sergeant Charles Church
John A. Clarke
Lewis Cobb
R. T. Coffey
Arthur B. Collom
Sergeant Arthur Cook
Jesse A. Cook
V. S. Crippen
Rex. Criswell, M
Homer Cross
Charles E. Curtis
David Davis
Corporal Hubert A. Dawson
Lieutenant Fred Dodge
Corporal Ray Eck
Fred Emerson
Corporal James Estalock
Ensign Hobart Fairman
Seibert Fairman
Lieutenant Henry C. Fisher
Sergeant Otto F. Fisher
Sergeant Floyd Fletcher
William T. Foreman
Arthur W. Foster
Ralph L. Foster
Sergeant Herbert A. Frazier
Lieutenant Dewey Fullington
T. O. Garringer
William Giles
Sergeant Howard Gingery
B. E. Gleason
*Lieutenant Ray F. Glover
Lieutenant Fred Griffee
Luke A. Guilfoyle
Sergeant John C. Gulledge
Corporal Edwin Gunn
F. L. Hall
*Sergeant Lester Hamil
Gordon W. Hamilton

Lieutenant Robert Hargis
Ernest Hartman
Edward Haug
Corporal Floyd Hawkins
Edwin C. Headley
Ethan A. Herr
Phillip G. Hill
Orrin W. Hinshaw
Dalton R. Hooton
Dick Hopper
James Huey
Stanley P. Hunt
Corporal Elmer C. Humphrey
E. W. Ikard
*Calvin L. Irwin
Lieutenant William C. Janssen
Corporal Myron Johnson
A. E. Jones
Lieutenant Francis M. Jordan
Lieutenant Horace L. Kapka
Corporal Walter Karlowski
*Lieutenant Clede R. Keller
Sergeant Robert Kilbourn
William Knostman
Dan G. Lake
Corporal Ira K. Landon
H. A. Lindsey
Coleman W. McCampbell
Lieutenant Elmer B. McCollum
Lieutenant R. Donald MacGregor
E. L. McIntosh
Calvin McInturff
*Sergeant Joseph H. McKee
Lieutenant Carl V. Maloney
Corporal Earle Manners
Earl J. Manninger
Lieutenant Schuyler Marshall
Ray Means
G. J. Mibeck
George A. Miller
H. P. Miller
J. G. Montague
Corporal J. Claire Morton
Sergeant Harry A. Muir
Charles H. Myers
Chester Neiswender
Clell A. Newell
R. D. Nichols
Sergeant Charles Nitcher
Lieutenant William A. Nye
Howard A. O'Brien
Charles O'Leary
Guy Oden
Henry Osoba
John S. Painter
Lieutenant Nevels Pearson
Orrin R. Peterson
William Pfaff
*Delbert Pollock
Corporal James E. Pratt
C. E. Prock
Leo Ptacek
Alfred K. Ramy

Sergeant William Rankin
Marion Reed
Lieutenant O. W. Reed
Lawrence Rayburn
E. H. Richardson
Frank L. Rimbach
Lieutenant Louis V. Ritter
Lloyd W. Roberts
Louis H. Rochford
Sergeant Carl O. Roda
Sergeant Clifford S. Rude
Homer Russell
Carew Sanders
H. Gordon Schultz
Lieutenant Elmer Schultz
Harry K. Shideler
Sergeant Clarence Sigler
Albert Sims
Corporal Orla D. Small
A. E. Smith
June B. Smith
W. E. Smith
Corporal C. W. Snodgrass
James Sparks
Sergeant Oscar Steanson
Sergeant Ralph Steffe
Lieutenant M. Stigers
Porrect Stone
Lowell Stone
Sergeant Ray H. Stratford
Lieutenant John G. Stutz
Arthur F. Swanson
Ray S. Talley
*Fred Taylor
Glenn Taylor
Lieutenant John E. Tillotson
Lewis Timons
L. A. Tilton
C. M. Tinkler
Gail M. Umberger
Mark Upson
Earl VanAntwerp
B. Vandiver
Ralph VanTrine
*Lieutenant Loyd Vorhies
Lieutenant George Washburn
R. J. Weinheimer
*Lieutenant Edward D. Wells
Sergeant Mark Wentz
R. S. Westcott
C. E. Wettig
Edwin F. Whedon
Sergeant Gilbert Whitsett
Laurence W. Wiest
E. T. Williamson
D. A. Wilson
Lieutenant Harberd A. Wise
Jay Woodhouse
Lawrence Woods
Irving Wulfekuhler
Lieutenant Theodore Yost
Sergeant Frank B. Young
Corporal Fred F. Young

---

*Deceased.

SOME OF THE 1919 MEN WHO SERVED. *Page 34*

Nevels Pearson

Turner Berger

Edward Haug

Nelson Anderson

Herbert Frazier

William A. Nye

Cecil L. Bower

SOME OF THE 1919 MEN WHO SERVED.

Fred Emerson

J. Clare Morton

Glenn Allen

Elmer C. Humphrey

Gilbert Whitsitt

Louis Ritter

W. C. Janssen

SOME OF THE 1919 MEN WHO SERVED.

Mark F. Upson

Hubert Dawson

Dewey Fullington

Lewis Timmons

Lowell M. Stone

Lewis Cobb

Laurence Wiest

SOME OF THE 1919 MEN WHO SERVED.

Henry Osoba

Ethan Allen Herr

Forrest Stone

Jesse Cook

William Rankin

Arthur Cook

Edward Wells

SOME OF THE 1919 MEN WHO SERVED

E. H. Chard

Fred Young

Gail Umberger

Bruce Brewer

Robert Kilbourn

Clifford Rude

Frank Young

SOME OF THE 1919 MEN WHO SERVED

To Those Who Helped

MOTHERS and fathers, we thank you for the splendid manner in which you have responded to our requests for pictures of your sons. For your interest and co-operation we owe you a lasting debt of gratitude.

Men of 1919, your enthusiasm and hearty support of the ROYAL PURPLE have been a constant source of inspiration to us. Whether your greetings came from France or from camps in our own United States, they brought with them good cheer and encouragement.

Editors.

WHO has not, especially in early youth, had a great desire to know big people personally? When we were little boys and girls, and went to community picnics, we stood quite in awe of the man who made the speech. The person in school who had shaken hands with the governor held enviable prestige.

Here at Kansas State we have come to know many great persons, and the realization of childhood ambitions has not been a disappointment. These men and women have given us the heritage of faith in life, for acquaintanceship has brought the realization that it is not money and brain that has made them great, but heart and soul.

PRESIDENT WILLIAM M. JARDINE

THE college catalogue gives President
Jardine's record such as college professors give
each other before making chapel speeches. It
lists his degrees and the places he has served.
It is enough for the students at Kansas State
to know that he is here now and that he holds a
master's degree in Aggie friendship and
democracy. There isn't a mean scared freshman who would be afraid to tell the president
his troubles.

DEAN JULIUS TERRASS WILLARD

Dean Willard is vice-president of the college, dean of the division of General Science and knows much about chemistry and other sciences. But we are interested in him because he is interested in us. We have a feeling that he is interested in our future careers. We know that five years from now a letter would find sympathetic audience and recognition in the office of Dean Willard.

DEAN MARY P. VAN ZILE

Dean Van Zile thoroughly understands.
She might have been a girl a very short time
ago for she knows just how we feel and think.
She is a jolly pal when we are good—but even
if we have done something rather awful we can
be sure that she will be fair and kind. These
are the qualities which make her worthy to be
dean of women.

DEAN HELEN B. THOMPSON

Dean Thompson is the efficient head of the Home Economics department. But one of the nicest things we know about her is that she sat and rooted for the Aggies through one football day that was so shivering cold there were few other women on the bleachers.

DEAN A. A. POTTER

The engineering men with one accord acclaim
their dean a good sport, which in college lan-
guage means much. Again there is a real man
back of national fame and achievement.

DEAN F. D. FARRELL

Dean Farrell educates farmers without
spoiling them. What better work could he do?

DEAN HARRY UMBERGER

At the head of the extension department,
Dean Umberger has the opportunity to take the
Kansas State Agricultural College to many
persons who cannot come to it. And he sends
the Aggie spirit free gratis.

DEAN H. L. KENT

Dean Kent gets jobs for us and he cares
what kind of a job it is.

J. R. McArthur

A. Dickens

R. R. Price

M. F. Ahearn

R. P. Dykstra

M. Sewell

C. F. Baker

Margaret H. Haggart

H. H. Ring

H. Durham

CLASSES

SENIORS

History of the Class of 1919

IN THE fall of 1915 there came to Kansas State College a group of talented youngsters who organized themselves into the Class of 1919. They chose as their motto, "Be on the job" and they have been on the job ever since.

Freshmen caps were worn religiously in 1915. In 1916 they were worn again but by the class of 1920. Why? Because the Class of 1919 saw to it that they were worn. Those were days of real sport down in Aggieville. More than one member of the Class of 1920 moved stiffly for a few days after the Class of 1919 had persuaded him to wear his perky little Freshman cap.

When Aggie Pop Night was invented by the Y. W. C. A. it was named so by one of the members of the Class of 1919. Grace Lightfoot's imagination and ingeniousness served her well, for Aggie Pop Night has played an important part in college activities. It was Rex Criswell who originated the idea of the Freshman-Sophomore Hop which is becoming a custom at Kansas State. It was the Class of 1919 that started the handing down of the Key to the Campus to the Freshmen each year at the Freshman-Sophomore Hop. It was a member of the Class of 1919 that suggested the all class election system which will probably become a custom at Kansas State. The idea of starting a fund for building a campanile on the campus also originated in this class.

When there came a call to the colors this class responded and many of its men went across, some never to return. Among these were Eddie Wells and Lloyd Vorhies. No men could be better liked or more respected than those two loyal Aggies who gave their lives for the sake of humanity.

The girls have done their share too. During the S. A. T. C., when the men were giving their time to their country, the girls took it upon themselves to keep the old time class spirit alive. Was there to be a class book? Of course. The girls were on the job and the 1919 Royal Purple is the result.

The college needed pep and there is nothing that brings the student body together more quickly than scandal sheets. Therefore there were scandal sheets of vivid hues. No one knows who printed these, but it isn't probable that the Class of 1919 let a chance go by for creating pep without having its finger in the pie.

Far be it from the Class of 1919 to seem conceited, for it is not. It is merely proud of its record, for it has a good record. Should the succeeding classes surpass this record we shall be only too glad to congratulate them. If they do not measure up to it we shall regret it.

—*Betty Cotton, Class Historian.*

Senior Class Officers

	First Semester	Second Semester
President	SARELLA HERRICK	GORDON HAMILTON
Vice-President	HAZEL TAYLOR	HATTIE DROLL
Secretary	MARTHA WEBB	LUCILE HALLECK
Treasurer	PEARL MILTNER	SEIBERT FAIRMAN

COMMITTEES

Senior Pin
LUCILE HEISER, Chairman

GAIL UMBERGER   LOLA SLOOP

Cap and Gown
HOMER CROSS, Chairman

MARTHA WEBB   GEORGE Y. BLAIR

Invitations
ELIZABETH COTTON, Chairman

C. H. MYERS   LUCILE HALLECK

Program
DONALD MACGREGOR, Chairman

MARY MASON   GUSSIE JOHNSON

Senior Play
GORDON HAMILTON, Chairman

VELMA CARSON   VERA SAMUELS

Class Memorial
BRUCE B. BREWER, Chairman

VERA OLMSTEAD   SEIBERT FAIRMAN

ALTO ADAMS   Lyons
   Home Economics
   Y. W. C. A.; W. A. A.

ELIZABETH ADAMS   Maple Hill
   Home Economics
   Pi Beta Phi; Y. W. C. A.; Hockey Team
      (1)

EDWIN O. ADEE   Manhattan
   Civil Engineering
   C. E. Society

JAMES BELL ANGLE   Courtland
   Animal Husbandry
   Alpha Theta Chi; Alpha Zeta; Quill;
      Saddle and Sirloin; Apollo Club

HARRY JONAS AUSTIN   Manhattan
   Veterinary Medicine
   Veterinary Medical Association

MADGE GLADYS AUSTIN   Manhattan
Home Economics
Ionian; Y. W. C. A.

TURNER BARGER   Newkirk, Okla.
Agronomy
Pi Kappa Delta; Athenian; Forum

IVYL BARKER   Newton
Industrial Journalism
Delta Delta Delta; Ionian; Quill

HUGH DONALD BARNES   Blue Mound
Civil Engineering
Hamilton; President Civil Engineers Society (3); Captain Class Football (2); Captain Engineer Football (3); Engineers' Basket Ball (3)

CARROLL BARRINGER   Conover, N. C.
Animal Husbandry
Sigma Nu; Hamilton; Saddle and Sirloin; Pax; Scarab; President of Class (3); Captain R. O. T. C.; Purple Masque; Lead in "Road to Yesterday"

ARTHUR ESCO BATE   Wichita
Veterinary Medicine
Sigma Phi Delta; Alpha Psi; Scarab;
Veterinary Medical Association.

F. R. BEAUDETTE   Wichita
Veterinary Medicine
Sigma Phi Delta; Veterinary Medical
Association

EDNA LOUISE BECKMAN   Manhattan
Home Economics
Y. W. C. A.

W. WALTON BELL   Marysville
Agronomy
Alpha Zeta; Athenian; Tri-K

GLADYS BERGIER   Manhattan
Home Economics
W. A. A.; Y. W. C. A.

MILDRED CONTENT BERRY   Jewell
Home Economics

Ionian; Omicron Nu; Y. W. C. A.

TRAFFORD WILLIAM BIGGER   Topeka
Mechanical Engineering

Sigma Tau; Alpha Beta; A. S. M. E.;
Engineering Association

EDITH FRANCES BIGGS   Dulce, N. Mex.
Home Economics

Pi Beta Phi; Y. W. C. A.

MARY AVIS BLAIN   Manhattan
General Science

Y. W. C. A.; Bethany Circle; W. A. A.;
Hockey Varsity (2, 3); Hockey
Captain (3, 4); Basket Ball (2, 3, 4);
Swimming Honors (1); Y. W. C. A.
Bible Study Committee; Junior
Farce (3)

GEORGE Y. BLAIR   Mulvane
Agronomy

Aztex; Alpha Zeta; Scarab; Pax; Theta
Sigma Lambda; Tri-K; Basket Ball
(4)

RUTH BLAIR   Hutchinson
Home Economics

Omicron Nu; Zeta Kappa Psi; Xix;
Ionian; Y. W. C. A.; Student
Council (4); Forum; Class Vice-
President (3); Royal Purple Staff;
Ionian Orator; Junior Farce

HELEN BLANK   Emporia
Home Economics

Pi Beta Phi; Y. W. C. A.; Enchiladas

SARAH JOANNA BOELL   Riley
General Science

Eurodelphian; Quill

FAYNE V. BONDURANT   Ness City
Home Economics

Chi Omega; Xix; Women's Pan-Hellenic;
Enchiladas; Y. W. C. A.

RUTH BORTHWICK   Independence
Home Economics

Alpha Delta Pi; Y. W. C. A.; Royal
Purple Staff, Editor Popularity
Section

BRI'CE BROWNE BREWER   Manhattan
Industrial Journalism

Sigma Nu; Sigma Delta Chi; Theta
Sigma Lambda; Pax; Scarab; Webster; Y. M. C. A.; President Class of
'19(2); Editor Kansas State Collegian (2, 3); Major R. O. T. C. (4);
Webster Orator (4)

SOLOMON RICHARD BRINKER   Greensburg, Pa.
General Science

Theta Xi

MARGARET SARA BROWNE   Burdett
Home Economics

Browning; Y. W. C. A.

RAVENA ELIZABETH BROWN   Lawrence
Home Economics

Eurodelphian; Y. W. C. A.; Big Sister
Captain

MILDRED C. BROWNING   Linwood
Home Economics

Browning; Y. W. C. A.

Lloyd H. Bunnel   Iola
 Agricultural Engineering
 Engineering Association

Phyllis Burt   Eureka
 Home Economics
  Kappa Kappa Gamma; W. A. A.;
  Enchiladas; Y. W. C. A.

Lois Ava Burton   Emporia
 Home Economics
  Chi Omega; Y. W. C. A.

Lucile Margaret Carey Manhattan
 Home Economics
  Browning; Y. W. C. A.

Velma Lenore Carson   Clifton
 Industrial Journalism
  Theta Sigma Phi; Ionian; Quill; Purple
  Masque; Y. W. C. A.; Prix; Xix;
  Oratorical Board; W. A. A.; Editor
  Royal Purple; Collegian Staff (3);
  Y. W. C. A. Cabinet (3); Class
  President (3); Cosmopolitan; Chair-
  man Junior Farce Committee; Pep
  Committee (3)

RAY TALLEY   Hutchinson
Architecture

IMOGENE MARJORIE CHASE   Manhattan
General Science
Y. W. C. A.

JOHN ALLEN CLARKE   Manhattan
Animal Husbandry

Aztex; Scarab; Theta Sigma Lambda; Varsity Foot ball (1, 2); Varsity Basket Ball (2, 3, 4); Varsity Baseball (2, 4); "K" Fraternity

RUSSELL F. COFFEY   Iola
Veterinary Medicine

Veterinary Medical Association; Vet Football (3); Vet Basket Ball (3)

JESSE ALFRED COOK   Eureka
Electrical Engineering

ELIZABETH COTTON   Wamego
  General Science

Kappa Kappa Gamma; Ionian; Forum;
    Xix; Prix; Y. W. C. A,; W. A. A.;
    Pan-Hellenic (2, 4); Manager Tennis
    Tournament (3); W. A. A. Council
    (3); Hockey (1, 3); Hockey Captain
    (2); Class Historian (3, 4); Class
    Editor, Royal Purple; Mathematical
    Club (1); Chairman Social Com-
    mittee (2); Junior-Senior Com-
    mittee (2); Kansas Executive Com-
    mittee Student Friendship War
    Fund (3); Chairman Invitation
    Committee (4); Y. W. C. A. Financial
    Committee (3); Y. W. C. A. Social
    Service Committee (4)

NADIA DUNN CORBY   Manhattan
  Industrial Journalism

Kappa Kappa Gamma; Theta Sigma Phi;
    Y. W. C. A.

VERNON SIMPSON CRIPPEN   Nickerson
  Agronomy

Tri-K; Athenian; Y. M. C. A.

HOMER CROSS   Wichita
  Electrical Engineering

Sigma Kappa Tau; Hamilton; Student
    President Y. M. C. A.; Junior
    Honors; R. O. T. C.; Engineering
    Association; A. I. E. E.; Oratorical
    Board; Pep Committee; Collegian
    Board

MARGARET ELIZABETH CRUMBAKER   Onaga
  Home Economics

Eurodelphian; Y. W. C. A.

MARY GRACE CRUMBAKER   Onaga
  Home Economics
  Eurodelphian; Y. W. C. A. Cabinet;
    Xix W. A. A.; Class Basket Ball

NORA MAY DAPPEN   Ramona
  General Science
  Y. W. C. A.

FLORENCE LILLIAN DIAL   Manhattan
  Home Economics
  Y. W. C. A.; St. Cecilia Club; W. A. A.

HATTIE E. DROLL   Wichita
  Home Economics
  Ionian; Y. W. C. A.; Xix; Y. W. C. A.
    Cabinet (2, 3, 4); Ionian Orator (2)

MINNIE DUBBS   Ransom
  Home Economics
  Franklin; Bethany Circle; Y. W. C. A.

LENORE EDGERTON   Randolph
   Home Economics
Delta Zeta

ANNA RUBY ELLERMAN   Potter
   Home Economics
Browning; Y. W. C. A.; W. A. A.

SEIBERT FAIRMAN   Manhattan
   Mechanical Engineering
Sigma Phi Epsilon; Pi Kappa Delta;
  Athenian; Scarab; Forum; A. S.
  M. E.; Engineers' Association; Band;
  K. K. Debater; Debate Council;
  Oratorical Board; Pentangular De-
  bate Team; Royal Purple Staff

MAURINE FITZGERALD   Colby
   Home Economics
Y. W. C. A.

BERTHA EDNA FLYNN   Humboldt
   Home Economics
 ' Eurodelphian; Y. W. C. A.

GEORGE ALBERT FOLTZ   Galveston, Tex.
  General Science

  Varsity Basket Ball (3, 4); Freshman
    Baseball; "K" Fraternity

W. THORNTON FOREMAN   Kiowa
  Electrical Engineering

  "K" Fraternity; Webster; Track (2, 3, 4);
    Captain Track (4); Engineering
    Association

SHIRLEY BLANCH FRENCH   Hamilton
  Animal Husbandry

  Delta Phi Delta

MURL GANN   Springfield, Mo.
  Home Economics

  Alpha Delta Pi; Y. W. C. A.; Girls' Pan-
    Hellenic Council; W. A. A.; Enchi-
    ladas

HATTIE PAULINE GESNER   Kiowa
  Home Economics

  Ionian; W. A. A.; Y. W. C. A.

HELEN ISABELL GOTT   Arlingto
Home Economics
    Franklin; Y. W. C. A.; St. Cecilia Clu▮
      Oratorical Board

EDWIN E. GOTTMAN   Kansas City, Ka▮
Dairy Husbandry
    Alpha Zeta

GREETA HAZEL GRAMSE   Perr▮
Home Economics
    Alpha Delta Pi; Eurodelphian; Purp▮
      Masque; Xix; W. A. A.; Deba▮
      Council (2); Inter-Society Counc▮
      (3, 4);Y.W. C. A. Cabinet (4);"Und▮
      Cover;" Treasurer Royal Purple

MYRTLE ANNICE GUNSELMAN   Holto
Home Economics
    Browning President (4); Forum Deba▮
      Council (3, 4), Vice-President (4); ▮
      W. C. A.; Inter-Collegiate Debate (▮

MARY FRANCIS HAACK   Florenc▮
Home Economics
    Delta Delta Delta; Y. W. C. A.

LUCILE HALLECK   Abilene
  Home Economics

Delta Delta Delta; Enchiladas; Y. W.
  C. A.; View Editor Royal Purple;
  Secretary Collegian Board (4); Xix

GORDON WILFRED HAMILTON   Salina
  Mechanical Engineering

Sigma Phi Delta; Sigma Tau; Pi Kappa
  Delta; Pax; Scarab; Hamilton;
  Forum; A. S. M. E.; Inter-Society
  Oratorical Contest (3); Class Presi-
  dent (4); Royal Purple Staff

ALICE TIBBETTS HARKNESS   Lakin
  Home Economics

Y. W. C. A.

EVA HARVEY   Osborne
  Home Economics

Browning; Bethany Circle; Y. W. C. A.

HELEN LUCILE HEISER   Tonganoxie
  Home Economics

Ionian President; Xix; Forum; W. A. A.
  President; Y. W. C. A. Cabinet;
  Student Council; Omicron Nu

RUTH B. HENDERSON   Alma
Industrial Journalism
Theta Sigma Phi

ALTA SARAH HEPLER   Manhattan
Home Economics
Browning; Y. W. C. A.

SARELLA LUCILE HERRICK   Topeka
Home Economics

Pi Beta Phi; Eurodelphian; Prix; Xix; Omicron Nu; Y. W. C. A.; Runner-up Tennis (2); Vanity Fair (3); Junior Honors; Pan-Hellenic Council (3); Secretary Y. W. C. A. Cabinet (3, 4); Treasurer Pep Committee (4); U. W. W. Executive Committee (4); Class President (4); Executive May Fete (3); Class Chairman Social Committee (3); Royal Purple Staff (4); Junior Farce

MARTIN EARLE HIESTAND   Yates Center
Agronomy
Tri-K; Athenian; Y. M. C. A.

CLARA E. HIGGINS   Hiawatha
Animal Husbandry
Tri-K; Y. W. C. A.; W. A. A.; College Orchestra

ORIN WILLARD HINSHAW   Eureka
   Horticulture
   Sigma Phi Epsilon

RUTH KATHRINA HUFF   Chapman
   Home Economics
   Franklin; Y. W. C. A.; W. A. A.; St.
     Cecelia Club (2, 3); Basket Ball
     (1, 2, 3, 4); Hockey Team (2, 3, 4)

STANLEY PAUL HUNT   Manhattan
   Mechanical Engineering
   Sigma Tau; A. S. M. E.; Engineers' As-
     sociation

ELIJAH HARRISON IKARD   Chickaska, Okla.
   Veterinary Medicine
   Alpha Psi; Veterinary Medical Asso-
     ciation; Vet Football (2); Vet Bas-
     ket Ball (3); Vet Baseball (3)

WILLIAM CURTIS JANSSEN   Lyons
   Agronomy
   Sigma Phi Epsilon; Alpha Zeta; Tri-K

GUSSIE C. JOHNSON   Wichita
Home Economics

Zeta Kappa Psi; Omicron Nu; Euro-
delphian; Forum; Prix; Xix; Y. W.
C. A. Debating Team (2); Royal
Purple Staff

JULIA ANNETTE KEELER   Luray
Industrial Journalism

Theta Sigma Phi

PHILLIP A. KENNICOTT, JR.   Woodbine
First Lieutenant in Cadet Corps

MAUDE EMILY KERSHAW   Garrison
Home Economics

Y. W. C. A.

ROBERT WARREN KILBOURNE   Sterling
Animal Husbandry

Athenian; Second Lieutenant of Cadet
Corps (2)

CHESTER A. KING   Emporia
  Veterinary Medicine (Pathology)
  Y. M. C. A.; S. A. T. C.; Veterinary
    Medical Association

MARY KIRKPATRICK   Holdrege, Neb.
  Chi Omega; Y. W. C. A.

EVALENE KRAMER   Washington
  Home Economics
  Delta Zeta; Xix; W. A. A.; Y. W. C. A.
    Enchiladas; Hockey (2, 3); Basket
    Ball (1)

ALPHA CORINNE LATZKE   Manhattan
  Home Economics
  Ionian; Omicron Nu; Y. W. C. A.

ESTHER NAOMI LATZKE   Manhattan
  Home Economics
  Ionian; Omicron Nu; Y. W. C. A.

LAVINIA LIEBENGOOD   Paola
Home Economics

HOWARD A. LINDSEY   Manhattan
    Dairy Husbandry; Shamrock; Dairy
    Association

OLIVE CHARLOTTE LOGERSTROM   Manhattan
    Home Economics
    Alpha Beta; Forum; Y. W. C. A.; Inter-
    Collegiate Debate; Oratorical Board
    (3, 4); Debate Council (2, 3)

C. W. McCAMPBELL   Corpus Christi, Tex.
    Agronomy
    Pi Kappa Alpha; Quill; Tri-K

HELEN McILRATH   Kingman
    Home Economics
    Ionian; Y. W. C. A.

IRMA ELLEN McKINNELL   Maize
   Home Economics

   Y. W. C. A.; W. A. A.; Hockey (2);
   Basket Ball (2, 3)

G. W. McCRACKEN   Holguin, Cuba
   Electrical Engineering

   Sigma Tau; Hamilton; Y. M. C. A.;
   I. E. E.; Engineering Association

JOHN L. McNAIR   Holmdel, N. J.
   Animal Husbandry

   Athenian; Saddle and Sirloin

ROBERT DONALD MacGREGOR   Topeka
   General Science

   Sigma Phi Epsilon; Pax; Scarab; "Man
     on the Box" (2); Pan-Hellenic
   Council (3, 4); First Lieutenant of
   Cadet Corps (3); Class Treasurer (3)

MARIE MANSER   Burden
   Home Economics

   Y. W. C. A.

MARTIN EDGAR   Siloam Springs, Ark.
Animal Husbandry
Elkhart Club; Y. M. C. A.

MARY MASON   Belle Plaine
Home Economics
Y. W. C. A. Cabinet; Eurodelphian;
Prix; Xix

LORAN GERTRUDE MENDANHALL
                            Fairbury, Neb.
Home Economics
Y. W. C. A.

GEORGE AARON MILLER   Portis
Mechanical Engineering
Hamilton

PEARL MILTNER   Wichita
General Science
Eurodelphian; Y. W. C. A.; Class
Treasurer (4); Junior Honors

MARY ETHEL MITCHELL   Emporia
Home Economics
Browning; Y. W. C. A.

LAURA DUELLE MOORE   Chanute
Industrial Journalism
Theta Sigma Phi; Winner of Industrialist
     Contest (3)

RUTH HILDA MOORE   Winfield
Home Economics
Pi Beta Phi; Y. W. C. A.

RUTH MORGAN   Neodesha
Home Economics
Y. W. C. A.

ALICE MORTON   Ellsworth
Home Economics

CLIFFORD HOWARD MYERS   Hutchinson
Mechanical Engineering

Beta Theta Pi; Pax; Scarab; Glee Club
(2, 3, 4), Cheer Leader (3, 4); Collegian Staff; Royal Purple Staff;
Pan-Hellenic Council

RALPH DALE NICHOLS   Manhattan
Animal Husbandry

Webster; Y. M. C. A.; Saddle and Sirloin

HOWARD ADAMS O'BRIEN   Luray
Veterinary Medicine

Sigma Nu; Alpha Psi; Veterinary Medical Association; Pax; Scarab; Class
Vice-President (4); Apollo Club
(2, 3, 4); "Sergeant Kitty" (3);
"Naughty Marietta" (4); President
of Collegian Board (4); Pan-Hellenic (3, 4); President of Medical
Section of S. A. T. C.

VERA OLMSTEAD   Moran
Home Economics

Ionian; Omicron Nu; Prix; Xix; Phi
Kappa Phi; Y. W. C. A. Cabinet (3, 4);
Business Manager of Royal Purple;
Junior Honors; Class Treasurer (4)

RUTH ORR   Manhattan
Home Economics

Omicron Nu

JOHN S. PAINTER   Beverly
     Electrical Engineering
     Sigma Tau; Hamilton; A. I. E. E.

BLANCH MARGUERITE PALMER
               Sterling, Colo.
     General Science
     Colorado College (1, 2); Y. W. C. A.

ROCCINA F. PARKER   Ottawa
     General Science
     Eurodelphian; Y. W. C. A.; W. A. A.

RAY REECE PARKER   Clearwater
     Veterinary Medicine
     Veterinary Medicine Association; Vet
       Football

RUTH ROSABELL PHILLIPS   Ottawa
     Home Economics
     Browning; St. Cecelia; Y. W. C. A.

FLOYD M. PICKRELL   Leon
Dairy Husbandry

Shamrock; Gamma Sigma Delta; Scabbard and Blade; Athenian; Apollo Club; Dairy Association

CHARLES EDWARD ZOLLINGER   Junction City
Veterinary Medicine

Alpha Psi; Veterinary Medical Association

EVERETT JACOB PRICE   Baileyville
Animal Husbandry

Alpha Zeta; Athenian; Saddle and Sirloin; Inter-Society Council (3, 4); Band

LOUIS VERNON RITTER   Memphis, Tenn.
Agronomy

Beta Theta Pi; Alpha Zeta; Scabbard and Blade; First Lieutenant of Cadet Corps; Winner of Stock Judging Contest (3); Winner of Clay Robinson Trophy on Sheep (3)

LLOYD WILLIAM ROBERTS   Pomona
Civil Engineering
Civil Engineering Society

LOUIS H. ROCHFORD   Osborne
   Animal Husbandry

   Sigma Alpha Epsilon; Purple Masque; Pax; Pan-Hellenic; Saddle and Sirloin

MAYBELL RODGERS   Cherryvale
   Home Economics
   Y. W. C. A.; W. A. A.

CLIFFORD SYMES RUDE   Manhattan
   General Science
   Athenian

FRANCES ELIZABETH RUSSELL   Scott City
   Home Economics
   Omicron Nu; Eurodelphian; Y. W. C. A.; Junior Honors

VERA LEONE SAMUEL   Iola
   Home Economics
   Omicron Nu; Xix; Browning; Bethany Circle; Y. W. C. A.; Student Council (4); Oratorical Board (4); Inter-Society Council (4)

ADDIE RUTH SANDMAN   Harbine, Neb.
  General Science
  Y. W. C. A.; W. A. A.

GORDON H. SCHULTZ   Manhattan
  Electrical Engineering
  Sigma Tau; Engineering Association;
    A. I. E. E.

ADELAIDE SEEDS   Topeka
  Home Economics
  Delta Delta Delta; Enchiladas; Y. W.
    C. A.

AUGUST ERNEST SCHATTENBURG Manhattan
  Veterinary Medicine
  Veterinary Medical Association

NELLIE G. SHOUP   Mulvane
  Home Economics
  Browning; Y. W. C. A.; Forum

LOLA MAE SLOOP   Boyle
Home Economics

Zeta Kappa Psi; Omicron Nu; Xix;
Browning; Forum; Y. W. C. A.;
Debate Council; Varsity Debate
(1, 2, 4); Winner of Women's De-
bating Scholarship (2, 3, 4); Royal
Purple Staff; Class Vice-President
(2); National President of Zeta
Kappa Psi

EVA JEANETTE SNYDER   Sterling
Home Economics

Cooper College (1, 2, 3); Y. W. C. A.

ESTHER ELIZABETH STONGE   Riley
Home Economics

Y. W. C. A.

MRS. MILLIE STEIN   Manhattan
Home Economics

ARTHUR FRITHIOF SWANSON   Manhattan
Agronomy

Pi Kappa Delta; Tri-K; Franklin;
Forum; Y. M. C. A.; Debating
Council (3); Inter-Society Debate
(2); Varsity Debate (2, 3); Franklin
Orator (4)

ETHEL GLADYS SWITZER   Emporia
Home Economics
   Franklin; Y. W. C. A.; Student Volun-
   teer

HAZEL DORA TAYLOR   Winfield
General Science
   Alpha Delta Pi; Xix; Y. W. C. A.;
   Mathematics Club; W. A. A.; Class
   Vice-President (4)

MARY F. TAYLOR   Newton
General Science
   Y. W. C. A.

RUTH G. TAYLOR   Tyro
Home Economics
   Chi Omega; Omicron Nu; Prix; Pan-
   Hellenic; Chairman Social Com-
   mittee (1); Class Secretary (1);
   Collegian Staff (3); Royal Purple
   Staff

EDITH TEAGUE   Collyer
Home Economics
   Y. W. C. A.

RUTH ELIZABETH THOMAS   Anthony
   Home Economics
   Prix; Xix; Eurodelphian; Y. W. C. A.;
      W. A. A.; Basket Ball Captain
      (1, 2, 3, 4); President W. A. A. (3);
      President Y. W. C. A. (4); Xix
      President (4)

L. A. TILTON   Bonner Springs
   Mechanical Engineering

GERTRUDE UHLEY   Fairbury, Neb.
   Home Economics
   Alpha Delta Pi; Y. W. C. A.

GAIL MORRIS UMBERGER   Elmdale
   Veterinary Medicine
   Alpha Psi; Scarab; Veterinary Medicine
      Association

AUROLYN AGNES VANDERVERT
                          Iowa City, Ia.
   Home Economics
   Iowa University (1, 2)

MYRTLE CORNELIA VANDERWILT   Solomon
Home Economics
Omicron Nu; Y. W. C. A.; Basket Ball (1)

ELIZABETH DORIS WADLEY
                    Kansas City, Kan.
Industrial Journalism
Collegian Staff (3); Collegian Editor (4)

MARTHA C. WEBB   Manhattan
Home Economics
Pi Beta Phi; Xix; Y. W. C. A.; W. A. A.;
Enchiladas; Pan-Hellenic; Class
Secretary (4); Basket Ball (3);
Royal Purple Staff

RALPH WESCOTT   Galena
Dairy
Shamrock; Dairy Club

EDWIN FREDERICK WHEDON
                    Sheridan, Wyo.
Aztex; Alpha Zeta; "K" Fraternity;
Scabbard and Blade; Tobasco; Sad-
dle and Sirloin; Pax Scarab; Cadet
Captain (2); Captain of Company
Winning Competitive Drill (2);
Varsity Football (2, 3); Varsity
Basket Ball (3); Varsity Track (3)

ERROL T. WILLIAMSON   Independence, Mo.
Electrical Engineering
Sigma Tau; Hamilton

FRANK C. WILSON   Manhattan
Agronomy

EDYTHE M. WILSON   Boulder, Colo.
Home Economics
Delta Zeta; W. A. A.; Y. W. C. A.;
Basket Ball (1, 2, 3, 4); Enchiladas;
W. A. A. Council (4); Hockey (2, 3,
4); Captain (3); Pan-Hellenic
Council (3, 4)

NETTIE WISMER   Pomona
General Science
Franklin; Y. W. C. A.; Hockey (4);
W. S. S. Campaign Committee

NELLIE FLO YANTIS   Manhattan
General Science
Ionian; Y. W. C. A.

SARA CHASE YOST   Manhattan
Industrial Journalism

Theta Sigma Phi; Ionian; Winner of Industrialist Contest (3); Junior Farce; Royal Purple Staff

FRANK B. YOUNG   Falfurrias, Tex.
Veterinary Medicine

Alpha Psi; "K" Fraternity; "B. A. B." Tobasco; Varsity Football (4); Veterinary Medical Association

FRED YOUNG   Manhattan
Dairy

Juniors

Class of 1920

Colors—Red and White.

WITH a strong determination to come back and win the fight for knowledge the class of 1920 responded noblv to the call. Ike Gatz was chosen president and under his leadership the campaign started with a zip. The first difficulty to be overcome was the "Stick Around Till Christmas" organization that insisted that military tactics came first and that knowledge held only second place. After much tactful maneuvering the situation was mastered and knowledge came out victorious. Once more steps were directed toward the Hall of Fame and then the "wicked chimmie" came along to distract attention. After a brief struggle it died an early death, and from then on Juniors walked the straight and narrow path toward finals.

Juniors have had fun and have enjoyed life. There have been ups and downs but they have put spice into the meetings. Next year they will mount the final steps to the Hall of Fame and as noble seniors will do their best to leave a mark as one of the live classes of K. S. A. C.

Junior Class Officers

FIRST SEMESTER

I. F. Gatz . . . . President
Edna Wilkin. . . . . . . Vice-President
Walter Carey . . . . . . Secretary
Helen Neiman . . . . Treasurer

SECOND SEMESTER

R. W. Hixon . . . . President
Anne Lorimer . . . . Vice-President
Irene Mott Guthrie . . . . . . Secretary
M. P. Schlaegel . . . . Treasurer

MABEL CHRISTMAS ADAMS   Garden City
Home Economics

IDA GERTRUDE ADEE   Manhattan
General Science

BOYD FUNSTON AGNEW   Yates Center
Agronomy

MILDRED ARENDS   Kansas City
Home Economics

EMMET S. BACON   Emporia
Veterinary Medicine

ESTHER GRACE BAYLES   Osage City
Home Economics

MABEL ROSE BENTLEY   Valhalla
Industrial Journalism

BERTHA BILTZ   Manhattan
Home Economics

NELSON BOYLE   Spivey
Animal Husbandry

KATHERINE BRANDNER   Everest
Home Economics

BERNARD B. BROOKOVER   Eureka
Animal Husbandry

OSCAR J. BROWN   Sanford, Fla.
Agronomy

CLARENCE LELAND BROWNING
Kingfisher, Okla.
Electrical Engineering

BESSIE CATHERINE BURKDOLL   Lane
Home Economics

HETTIE CARRIS   Topeka
Home Economics

DORA L. CATE   Manhattan
Industrial Journalism

ELIZABETH CIRCLE   Kiowa
General Science

FRANK H. COLLINS   Wellsville
General Science

WARREN EUGENE CRABTREE　　Scott City
Animal Husbandry

DORIS M. CRANDALL　　Manhattan
Home Economics

RUBY LEE CROCKER　　Matfield Green
Industrial Journalism

MAY DAHNKE　　Manhattan
Home Economics

VERLA DAHNKE　　Manhattan
Home Economics

BERTHA DANHEIM　　Manhattan
Home Economics

HELEN J. DAWLEY   Manhattan
Home Economics

LULU ELIZABETH DEIST   Harper
Home Economics

LAURA VIOLA DENMAN   Manhattan
General Science

CHARLES BODDIE DOWNER   Kansas City
Electrical Engineering

VINNIE DRAKE   Manhattan
Home Economics

MYERS DUPHORNE   Sharon Springs
Electrical Engineering

HAZEL VIOLA DYER   Oberlin
Home Economics

SIEBERT ERIKSEN   Kensal, N. Dak.
Veterinary Medicine

MARGARET ETZOLD   Liberal
Home Economics

PAUL L. FETZER   Helena, Okla.
Mechanical Engineering

INA RUTH FINDLEY   Manhattan
Home Economics

ELOISE FLANDERS   Westboro, Mo.
Home Economics

MARY ABBIGAIL FURNEAUX   Moran
Home Economics

GLADYS GANSHIRD   Manhattan
Home Economics

ISAAC GATZ   Inman
Veterinary Medicine

MARIE GEHR   Manhattan
Home Economics

LESTER F. GFELLER   Junction City
Electrical Engineering

GRACE IOLA GISH   Manhattan
General Science

RUTH STEPHENS GOODRUM   Lamar, Mo.
Home Economics

RUTH GHORMLEY   Partridge
Home Economics

MARY RUTH GORHAM   Garden City
Home Economics

MAMIE GRIMES   Manhattan
Home Economics

JOHN F. GRADY   Lansing
Civil Engineering

IRENE MOTT GUTHRIE   Herington
Home Economics

EVA MAUD GWIN   Washington
Home Economics

FRED L. HALL

MARIE HAMMERLY   Manhattan
Home Economics

C. G. HANSEN   Sedgwick
Mechanical Engineering

CLAUDE B. HARRIS   Havensville
Agronomy

MARIE ELLEN HAYNES   Emporia
Home Economics

JESSIE HIBLER   Springfield, Mo.
   Home Economics

HARRY BERNICE HICKMAN   Norton, Mo.
   Veterinary Medicine

MARY JANE HILL   Burlington
   Home Economics

RALPH HIXON   Hiawatha
   Veterinary Medicine

LESTER H. HOFFMAN   Abilene
   Electrical Engineering

S. W. HONEYWELL   Manhattan
   Electrical Engineering

W. H. HORLACKER

HAZEL DELL HOWE   Garrison
    Home Economics

STUART L. HUNT   Blue Rapids
    Veterinary Medicine

JANE JENKINS   Manhattan
    Home Economics

HELEN M. JOHNSON   Wichita
    Home Economics

SAMUEL RAY JOHNSON   Coin, Ia
    Veterinary Medicine

MARY CATHERINE JOHNSTON   Gardner
    Home Economics

MARIE JULIAN   Hastings, Neb.
    Home Economics

ELITHE ELECTA KAULL   Kansas City
    General Science

GEORGE LOWELL KELLEY   White Cloud
    Agronomy

CLIFFORD KNISELEY   Wichita
    Mechanical Engineering

HELEN LAWRENCE   Junction City
    Home Economics

ANNE M. LORIMER   Olathe
  Home Economics

GLADYS LOVE   Kansas City, Mo.
  Home Economics

FRANCES EVELYN LOVETT   Eureka
  Home Economics

MERLE JAMES LUCAS   Pratt
  Electrical Engineering

EUGENE SIDNEY LYONS   Lawrence
  Agronomy

L. A. MAGRATH   Williamsburg
  Veterinary Medicine

MEDLIN   Manhattan
ial Journalism

SERVE   Ellis
Economics

*LETON   Minneapolis
Economics*

ERSON MILLER   Belleville
ial Journalism

*MILLER   Neodesha
Economics*

MILLER   Belleville
ngineering

JOSEPHINE MELDRUM   Cedar Vale
    Home Economics

FLORENCE IRENE MIRICK   Otis
    Home Economics

EDITH MUIR   Salina
    Home Economics

JOSEPH LINN MULLEN   Clay Center
    Animal Husbandry

BARBARA ELIZABETH MURRAY   Ash Grove
    Home Economics

HELEN ISABEL NEIMAN   Whitewater
    Home Economics

NELLIE M. PAYNE   Manhattan
General Science

DORIS HAWTHORNE PRICKETT Wamego
Home Economics

EDNA WINIFRED PYLE   Morrill
Home Economics

PHOEBE FRANCES REBSTOCK   Newton
Home Economics

ELIZABETH RITTER   Manhattan
Home Economics

ADA LA VERNE ROBERTSON   Washington
Home Economics

W. E. ROBISON   Towanda
Animal Husbandry

WALTER WILLIAM RODEWALD   Halstead
Agronomy

ANNA MARIE ROENIGK   Morganville
Home Economics

LENORA OLIVE RUDE   Manhattan
General Science

FRANK LOUIS SAHLMANN   Manhattan
Electrical Engineering

BLANCH SAPPENFIELD   Abilene
General Science

JEWELL SAPPENFIELD   Abilene
    General Science

LUELLA SCHAUMBURG   LaCrosse
    Agronomy

MERRILL PHILLIP SCHLAEGEL   Olsburg
    Veterinary Medicine

WILLIAM DENNIS SCULLY   Belvue
    Engineering

HELEN SLAVENS   Kansas City, Mo.
    Home Economics

PRUDENCE STANLEY   Topeka
    Home Economics

GRACE K. SMITH   Le Roy
    Home Economics

ELLA BELLE STINSON   Kansas City
    Home Economics

T. T. SWENSON   Lindsborg
    Animal Husbandry

JOSEPHINE SULLIVAN   Wamego
    Home Economics

L. BRAINARD TAYLOR   Arkansas City
    Veterinary Medicine

DONALD THAYER   Manhattan
    Agronomy

THOMPSON   Densmore
al Husbandry

A. THRESHER   Jetmore

RACE   Manhattan
omy

ROUTFETTER   Colby
al Science

RA TURNER   Milton
omy

EAL WATERS   Blue Rapids
omy

M. W. WATT   Topeka
   Agronomy

LAVERNE WEBB   Cedar Vale
   Home Economics

EDITH WHEATLEY   Rosedale
   Home Economics

B. B. WHITE   Delphos
   Veterinary Medicine

ANDREW WILBUR WILCOX   Manhattan
   General Science

ALMA WILKIN   Manhattan
   Home Economics

EDNA WILKINS   Manhattan
Home Economics

HOMER BRYAN WILLIS   Manhattan
Animal Husbandry

FAYE WILLIAMS   Gardner
Home Economics

HOMER CARLTON WOOD   Manhattan
Agronomy

MARGARET WOODMAN   Manhattan
Industrial Journalism

HAROLD STEPHEN WOODARD   Glen Elder
Animal Husbandry

CLARK O. WORKS   Humboldt
Agronomy

FLOYD WORKS   Windom
Mechanical Engineering

FAY A. YOUNG   Burlington
Home Economics

VERA CATES   Manhattan
Home Economics

DORA GROGGER   Manhattan
Home Economics

RUTH ANNA HARDING   Marion
Home Economics

BERTHA ELIZABETH GLENN   Manhattan
Home Economics

BESSIE LYMAN   Manhattan
Home Economics

GARNETT W. REED   Kansas City, Mo.
General Science

AMANDA ROSENQUIST   Osage City
Home Economics

CHARLOTTE RUSSELL   Manhattan
Industrial Journalism

W. G. WISE

Sophomores

The Class of 1921

THE FALL of 1918 with the whole student body under military regulations was perhaps the hardest season the classes of K. S. A. C. have ever seen within the last decade. Many of our strongest men were taken right out of class ranks and put into military camps. The student soldiers were kept too close to the barracks to take any part in class affairs. The "flu" made many of these men its victims and broke into school two different times. Finally, though, girls were elected to the responsible offices and came to the rescue of class affairs. From that election on, things have run quite smoothly.

The Sophomores had a very nice dance during the first semester and indulged in the usual sport of intruding at Freshmen parties.

The Class of '21 is well represented in basket ball, football, debate, dramatics and several other college activities. They have just had a very successful and peppy election and are making live plans for the rest of this year.

𝕾𝔬𝔭𝔥𝔬𝔪𝔬𝔯𝔢 𝕮𝔩𝔞𝔰𝔰 𝔒𝔣𝔣𝔦𝔠𝔢𝔯𝔰

FIRST SEMESTER

MARY DUDLEY	*President*
CHRISTINE COOL	*Vice-President*
RUBY CANADAY	*Secretary*
EVERETT WILLIS	*Treasurer*

SECOND SEMESTER

HARTZELL BURTON	*President*
MARY FRANCES DAVIS	*Vice-President*
JOSEPHINE SHUMAKER	*Secretary*
MERTON OTTO	*Treasurer*

EARL G. ABBOTT   GEORGE CLARENCE ANDERSON   MINNIE AUGUSTINE
KATHARIN RUTH ADAMS   ARDIS ATKINS

CHARLOTTE H. AYERS   FLORENCE BANKER   EDNA M. BARNES
JEAN BAKER   PAUL W. BARBER

HARVEY BARNES   LINDLEY C. BINFORD   ELSA A. BROWN
WILLIAM BERGH   VIOLA BRAINARD

J. FARR BROWN   GLADYS E. BUSHONG   JAMIE CAMERON
HOLMAN L. BUNGER   REX D. BUSHONG

RUBY M. CANADAY   MARION C. CLARKE   CARL M. CONRAD
HORTENSE CATON   MARY COFFMAN

CHRISTINE C. COOL   GEORGE CROUSE   ABBIE C. DENNEN
HUBERT J. COUNSELL   OSCAR L. CULLEN

DORSIE L. DENISTON   ANSEL C. BROWNING   CHESTER H. ELDER
ADDISON C. DEPEW   MARY E. DUDLEY

K. RICHMOND ELLIOT   JESSIE B. EVANS   ARTHUR M. FINE
MILDRED F. EMRICK   [OR] BLY EWALT

GLADYS FLIPPO   CONNIE C. FOOTE   O. D. GARDNER
HAZEL M. FLOWER   GLADYS E. FORD

RUTH GARVIN   EUGENE E. GILBERT   RUTH H. GILLES
S. J. GILBERT   HELEN L. GILES

EDWARD G. GIRARD   IRENE F. GRAHAM   BERTHA M. GWIN
DOROTHY A. GLEASON   HILBORN H. GROAT

ISABEL HAMILTON   MARGUERITE HAMMERLI   EMMA HERREN
LLOYD L. HAMILTON   RUTH G. HARRISON

EDITH L. HOAG   IRENE HOFFINES   FLORA PEARL HOOTS
FRANK HOATH   ARLINE A. HONEYWELL

W. HAROLD HOOTS   CLARA B. HOWARD   CHARLES W. HOWE
MARION C. HAUGHTON   DAVID M. HOWARD

OLIVER D. HOWELLS   DAN L. JANTZ   GERTRUDE LUCY JENNINGS
MAY HUNTER   EDWARD J. JELDEN

Henrietta Jones   Katherine Kinman   Esther L. Kohler
Everett B. Kain   Bernice Klotz

Inez Lake   Ione E. Leith   Carroll L. Lund
Clara I. Larson   Lucile Luderickson

Geta Lund   R. W. McCall   W. L. McGehee
N. D. Lund   Winifred O. McCarty

CHARLES C. McPHERSON   MARGUERITE MILLER   GEORGE M. MUNSELL
MARVEL MERILLAT   J. MARSHALL MILLER

G. HAROLD MOLESWORTH   DOROTHY MOSLEY   MARRIANE H. MUSE
LUELLA MORRIS   DONALD JOSEPH MOSEHART

ALICE MUSTARD   FRANCIS JOSEPH MIDDLETON   MERTON L. OTTO
OLIVER FRANKLIN NELSON   R. C. NICHOLS

EXENE OWENS   FAYE M. POWELL   EDITH RALSTON
LEE M. PARRISH   ELVA PRICE

FLORENCE E. REINER   KATHARINE RODERICK   GLADYS ROSS
NELL ROBINSON   ETHEL ROOP

DOROTHY RYHARD   BENNIE SCHEMONSKI   CRISTEL ATCHISON
MARION E. SANDERS   ABRAHAM BURTON SCHMIDT

MARCIA A. SEEBER   OURSULA S. SENN   JOSEPHINE SHUMAKER
    CAROLINE M. SEITZ   CLARE L. SHELLENBERGER

HELEN SLOAN   CLARA M. SMITH   N. S. SPANGLER
    CAROLINE SLOOP   LUELLA M. SNAY

VICTOR COSAD   ELMA STEWART   E. A. TUNNICLIFFE
    WILLIAM T. STERLING   J. E. THACKERY

Grace L. Turner   Hazel M. Watson   Sara Weide
Mattie E. Washburn   Norine Weddle

Frances Westcott   Ruth Willis   J. C. Wilson
J. F. Williams   Charles T. Wilson

Lee Winter   Esther Wright
Warren Woodman   L. D. Zimmerman

Sophomore Women's Athletics

BASKET BALL TEAM

HOCKEY TEAM

FRESHMEN

Freshman Class Officers

FIRST SEMESTER

DEWEY HUSTON	*President*
VOREN WAUGHN	*Vice-President*
MARJORIE FISHER	*Secretary*
GAIL LYNCH	*Treasurer*

SECOND SEMESTER

MIKE PTACEK	*President*
MORRIS SALISBURY	*Vice-President*
BURDETTE TEGMIER	*Secretary*
T. RAYMOND	*Treasurer*

SOME OF THE FRESHMEN

Freshman Athletics

THE COLLEGE MAY GO WILD OVER THEM SOME DAY

Class History of the School of Ag.

THIS, the Class of 1919, is the fifth class of the School of Agriculture to graduate from the vocational course connected with K. S. A. C. The class early formed an organization with Robert Keys as president. The first social function was a mixer held in the Domestic Science building and this brought about amity and good fellowship. A remarkable amount of interest was shown in athletics in the school of agriculture in the year of 1916-17. There were boys' and girls' basket ball teams and a girls' hockey team which won the hockey championship of K. S. A. C.

During the second year the class organization lapsed, but a mixer was held in the spring. The third and the last year began with enthusiasm with Ben Thompson as president. Two all-school of Agriculture social functions were held. The first was a mixer in the gymnasium under the chairmanship of Miss Orem and J. R. Smithheizer. Every one who was present will testify they spent a very enjoyable evening. The other was a party on the Country Club grounds under the chairmanship of Herman Metz. This was one of the most successful events of the year.

Most of the class are members of one or the other of the two literary societies from which they gain much in literary training and leadership. Joint programs, spelling matches, hikes and the annual taffy pull, being some of the events of the year.

The days spent in the School of Agriculture will always be among the happiest.

Graduating Class of the School of Agriculture

ALICE L. BOBECK, Caldwell
Home Economics

IRENE PIERATT, Hartford
Home Economics

STELLA HORCHEM, Ramona
Y. W. C. A., Philomathean
Home Economics

MARY L. BLUE, Detroit
Y. W. C. A.
Home Economics

EMILIO V. GOMEZ, San Antonio, Texas
Y. M. C. A., Cosmopolitan Club, School
of Ag. Football (1916)
Agriculture

THOMAS G. BETTS, Detroit
Lincoln Literary Society
Mechanical Arts

R. V. BARRINGTON, Sedan
Lincoln Literary Society, Y. M. C. A.
Agriculture

LOIS SCHLAEGEL, Olsburg
Philomathean Literary Society, Y. W.
C. A.
Home Economics

BEN A. THOMPSON, Densmore
Lincoln, Class President, Students' Coun-
cil, Elkhart
Agriculture

CORDELIA MASTERSON, Corning
Home Economics

MILITARY

Aggie Men Were Ready

WHEN war clouds, which had been threat-
euing the nation for two years, finally broke
on April 6, 1917, the United States found itself in a
pitiful state of unpreparedness. There was a hustle
to send men to officers' training camps, to build
cantonments, to plan for a new air service, to provide
for supplies and to organize generally for a vigorous
offensive in France.

One group of civilians, however, was partially
prepared. These men were the alumni and under-
graduates of Kansas State—men who had learned
the fundamentals of drill on the slope east of the
auditorium. These trained Aggies responded splendidly, and proved by their rapid promotions that
military training in the college—training which
Aggie men had been given for years—had prepared
them to face squarely the problems of war.

The fall of 1918 found the former Reserve Officers' Training Corps replaced by the Students' Army
Training Corps. The College campus was alive
with khaki-clad men and every day found them
busy with study and drill.

In the following pages an effort is made to por-
tray a bit of the military side of college life at
K. S. A. C.

CAPTAIN GEORGE STURGES

received his commission from the second officers' training camp, Camp Grant, Illinois. He was assigned to Camp Funston, where he was with the 353rd Infantry. Captain Sturges came to K. S. A. C. as commanding officer of the first training detachment, and later commanded both sections of the S. A. T. C.

CAPTAIN STURGES

CAPTAIN KEMPER

CAPTAIN RALPH L. KEMPER

received his commission from the second officers' training camp, Fort Benjamin Harrison, Indiana. He was first sent to Camp Funston, where he served with the Machine Gun Company of the 353rd Infantry. He came to K. S. A. C. with Captain Sturges, and later was in charge of Section B of the S. A. T. C.

Part Played by the S. A. T. C.

THE OUTSTANDING FEATURE of the military work of this year unquestionably consists in the organization and experience of the collegiate section of the Students' Army Training Corps, briefly designated as Section A, S. A. T. C. Units of this corps were organized in more than six hundred educational institutions. The general purpose was to give practical military training, together with instruction in subjects of military value, to a large body of men, many of whom would be good officer material.

From May 15 to June 15 the college trained in half a dozen vocational mechanical lines a detachment of two hundred and fifty drafted men. From July 15 to September 15 a second detachment of five hundred men received similar instruction and about September 15 a third detachment arrived for such instruction. On October 1, 1919, the training detachment of five hundred men became the vocational section, or Section B of the S. A. T. C., and on the same date the collegiate section was inducted into the service. Impressive ceremonies were held on the slope east of the auditorium.

College had opened on September 9 and in preparation for the collegiate section of the S. A. T. C., all young men in college curricula who desired to enter the corps were given assignments in harmony with instructions from the War Department. The committee of the War Department, however, issued orders later which made it necessary to change the assignments of a large number of the students who were twenty years or more of age. These and other orders from the department were cheerfully complied with.

By an order of the State Board of Health the college was closed on account of the epidemic of influenza from October 12 to November 10. Shortly after the closing of the college the influenza broke out among the soldiers, and the military medical officers, assisted by other physicians, Red Cross nurses, and volunteer nurses from the ladies of the faculty and of Manhattan, were taxed to the utmost to care for the sick. At the height of the epidemic six fraternity houses and the Y. M. C. A. building, all of which had been in use as barracks, were required for hospital purposes. Two hundred and fifty-seven of the collegiate section suffered from the disease. Four of these died. In Section B there were two hundred and thirteen cases with six deaths. Comparatively few students outside of the corps were effected. A second outbreak of the influenza in the city caused another closing of the college by order of the local board of health from December 9 to December 30.

With the signing of the armistice November 11 the interest of the students in the S. A. T. C. and in military work slackened, and the interference of military routine with college duties and privileges was felt to a great extent. The corps was demobilized within a period of a few days beginning December 10.

Some of the S. A. T. C. Officers

CAPTAIN WILLIAM B. PETERS

LIEUTENANT FRANCIS E. BROLLIAR

LIEUTENANT HARRY M. CLEVELAND

LIEUTENANT ERNEST M. COLE

LIEUTENANT CLAUDE V. COCHRAN

LIEUTENANT JOHN E. SMITH

LIEUTENANT EDWIN M. TAYLOR

LIEUTENANT JESSE ROSENBAUM

Company One

Company One

CO. 2 B SECTION S.A.T.C. KANSAS STATE AGRICULTURAL COLLEGE

Company Two

Company Three

Company Three

Company Four

Company Four

Company Five

Company Five

THE BATTALION IN FORMATION

AGGIE MEN MOLDED INTO LETTERS

Building the Barracks

When the men of the first training detachment arrived on the college campus on May 15, 1918, the authorities were without barracks in which to house the newcomers. The only available accommodations were in the college gymnasium. Those in charge decided to use this building as temporary quarters, and the "gym" became the home of the two hundred fifty men of the first detachment. The regular college activities for which the gymnasium is ordinarily used were dispensed with, and the immense room was lined with rows of cots.

This housing provision was merely temporary and as soon as possible barracks were to be constructed. Preliminaries were completed and the actual construction of the first building was begun on June 10.

That part of the campus where the new barracks were to be located took on new life. A large number of workers were employed and every day they were busily engaged in the construction of the soldiers' quarters. Steadily the work proceeded and with as great rapidity as could be expected. By the middle of July, little more than a month after operations had been begun, the first barracks was completed. At the same time five hundred new men were sent to begin the vocational course. The one building which had just been completed could accommodate only one hundred fifty men. One hundred soldiers were housed in the largest recitation room of the shop building and the remainder were quartered in the gymnasium.

The building of the other barracks was pushed as fast as possible. On August 8 the second building was completed and ready for occupancy.

The soldiers were moved out of their temporary quarters and into the barracks as rapidly as these buildings were completed. On August 11 the mess hall was ready for operation and five hundred men were served there. Before this time a large number had been given meals in the college cafeteria building. By September 10, the beginning of the college year,  four large barracks had been erected and were occupied by men of the training detachments. This meant that the work had been done in surprising time—three months. When the college students returned they found that this new group of buildings had sprung up on the campus like a mushroom growth. The last barracks, the fifth one, was completed by the first of October, when the collegiate and vocational sections of the newly organized Students' Army Training Corps were inducted into the service. As many as possible of the student soldiers were housed in the barracks on the campus, the remainder being assigned to certain houses in town which had been turned over to the S. A. T. C. There were two mess halls on the campus, and they were large enough to accommodate all the men.

In addition to these buildings, a "Y Hut" was constructed by the Young Men's Christian Association. This was near the barracks. It was not completed, however, until after the signing of the armistice. Its purpose was the same as that of all other huts of the same organization—to give the soldiers a place in which to read and write, and spend any leisure minutes which they might have.

THE SOLDIER BLACKSMITHS AT WORK

UNCLE SAM'S AUTO MECHANICS

Long Point 1-2   On Guard

Up and At 'Em   Going Over the Top   No Mans Land

Long Point in Action   Short Point

Reforming the Line

In Blues and —

In Whites

Ready for Huns

Woody

Scrub 'Em Up

These Helped Pershing

An Air Battler

Don Hughes   "A²" Grant

Sailing High

Washburn   Charley Enlow

The Officers in Charge

MAJOR DAVIDSON

CAPTAIN KEMPER

A T THE beginning of the second semester, when the Reserve Officers' Training Corps was to be organized, Captain Ralph Kemper, the only officer remaining from the Students' Army Training Corps group, took charge temporarily. He divided the corps into four companies. Soon, however, Major L. C. Davidson, a West Point graduate who had been with the Forty-first Infantry at Camp Funston, was detailed as Commandant and Professor of Military Science and Tactics. He organized the advanced classes of the corps, and picked out cadet officers to take charge of the companies.

The work of these two men has been important in the good results obtained in the short time that the R. O. T. C. was functioning. Both are young and have plenty of initiative. These qualities, together with the ability of both officers to get into close touch with the students, made them popular with the men in the corps.

The student heads of the corps are Bruce B. Brewer, senior in industrial journalism, who is cadet major, and Raymond C. Plyley, first lieutenant and battalion adjutant. Mr. Plyley is a junior in engineering. E. C. Waters is the battalion sergeant-major.

The Reserve Officers' Training Corps

T HE RESERVE OFFICERS' TRAINING CORPS was organized by the government to provide for a supply of reserve officers in time of war. Unfortunately, the system had been in operation only a short time and in only a few colleges when America was plunged into war with the Central Powers, and a supply of trained men with which to officer the troops was not available. Even in the short time that the plan had been in operation however, wonderful results were obtained, and a limited supply of students were commissioned directly from the corps.

The R. O. T. C. was established at the Kansas State Agricultural College at the beginning of the spring semester, 1918. A regimental organization was perfected under Captain W. P. J. O'Neill, an officer detailed by the War Department. At the beginning of the fall semester, 1918, the R. O. T. C. gave way to the Students' Army Training Corps, an organization with a larger and broader officers' training plan. This student army was demobilized following the signing of the armistice, November 11, 1918, and at the beginning of the spring semester, 1919, the R. O. T. C. came back into its own.

Major L. C. Davidson was detailed as Commandant and Professor of Military Science and Tactics, and Captain Ralph L. Kemper, a former S. A. T. C. officer, remained to assist Major Davidson.

Military Science as taught under orders from the War Department is divided into classes, with each college group studying different subjects. All students in the corps drill two hours each week. During the present semester this practical work has been given during the first and second hours on Monday morning. Then the groups of underclassmen are split up to receive an hour of instruction during the week under Captain Kemper.

Juniors and Seniors who elect to take the advanced courses are grouped into classes under Major Davidson. All officers are picked from the upperclassmen, and these assemble immediately following the drill period for a discussion with the Commandant of problems which arose during the drill, and of the plans for the following week. Aid in giving commands is also a part of this hour's instruction.

In the advanced courses are taught such subjects as the general military policy of the United States, principles of military combat, camp sanitation, recent military history, technical problems in patrolling and in advance, rear and flank guards, trench warfare, minor warfare, camp expedients, marches and camps, orders and messages, field orders, map maneuvers, company administration, minor tactics, elements of international law, property accountability and methods of obtaining supplies and property.

Students in all courses receive one complete woolen uniform each year. Rifles, bayonets and other ordnance materials are furnished by the government. Students who elect to attend a one month's summer camp receive commutation of subsistence, amounting to approximately twelve dollars for each of twelve months.

H.S. Woodward
Captain

J.E. Thackerey
First Lieut.

N.W. Watt
Second Lieut.

R.C. Plyly
First Lieut. Battalion Adjutant

W.J. Bucklee.
First. Lieut.

D.N. Keas
Second Lieut.

C.C. McPherson
Captain

D.C. Thayer
Captain

R.D. Hilliard
First Lieut.

C.E. Hutto
Second Lieut.

B.B. Brewer
Major

W.C. Wilson
First Lieut.

W.F. Hawkins
Second Lieut.

W.D. Scully
Captain

Company A

CADET CAPTAIN
D. C. THAYER

CADET LIEUTENANTS
R. D. HILLIARD, *First Lieutenant*   C. E. HUTTO, *Second Lieutenant*

CADET SERGEANTS
A. A. GRAVES, *First Sergeant*   J. W. BARGER, *Supply Sergeant*
K. C. FRANK   C. WEBER

CADET CORPORALS

G. GLENDENNING	C. E. GRAVES	R. S. CIRCLE
L. BYERS	G. E. FINDLEY	W. COWELL

CADET PRIVATES

C. E. AGNEW	R. BRADLEY	C. C. DETHLOFF
J. H. ALBRIGHT	C. BRADSHAW	L. A. DUMOND
DALE ALLEN	H. L. BROWN	C. S. EBENSTEIN
J. L. ALLEN	O. K. BRUBAKER	L. M. EDDY
H. ANDERSON	L. BUMGARDNER	V. J. ENGLAND
P. ANTHONY	E. F. BURK	E. R. ENNS
A. L. AUSTIN	G. H. BUSH	K. C. FARLEY
O. H. AYDELOTTE	O. BUTLER	P. FOLTZ
E. BAILEY	V. A. CHASE	E. GARD
M. H. BANKS	F. CHRISTMAN	G. L. GARLOCK
F. L. BARTLETT	R. E. CLEGG	G. E. GATES
C. O. BECKETT	F. COCHERELL	W. B. GLENN
J. A. BELLOMY	H. COFFMAN	E. F. GRAVES
WM. BERGH	R. COOPER	SHANNON BROWN
C. E. BLECKLEY	D. K. COPELAND	

Company B

CADET CAPTAIN
W. D. Scully

CADET LIEUTENANTS
W. C. Wilson, *First Lieutenant*   W. F. Hawkins, *Second Lieutenant*

CADET SERGEANTS
D. E. Houston, *First Sergeant*   P. C. Manglesdorf, *Supply Sergeant*
H. E. Howard   W. A. Lobaugh

CADET CORPORALS

E. J. Jelden	R. E. Marshall	G. T. James
T. R. Griest	G. M. Longley	L. D. Leach

CADET PRIVATES

A. E. Green	H. Hudson	J. A. McKittrick
E. Griffith	H. B. Hunt	P. M. McKown
H. H. Groat	J. C. Jones	J. T. Mackay
J. E. Haag	H. J. Kapka	A. Meade
N. A. Hammond	O. H. Karns	R. L. Meyer
B. Hefling	P. Kovar	J. M. Miller
N. W. Heim	F. Larner	Cecil Moore
J. J. Hendrix	L. M. Leiter	C. R. Moore
J. Hill	L. S. Lemert	G. D. Morris
E. E. Hodgson	D. G. Lynch	G. Murray
E. Hokanson	Wade McFarland	N. S. Nay
B. O. Holland	H. T. McKeever	W. Nordstrom
K. Houser	C. H. Howe	L. F. Patten

Company C

CADET CAPTAIN
H. S. WOODARD

CADET LIEUTENANTS
J. E. THACKEREY, *First Lieutenant*   M. W. WATT, *Second Lieutenant*

CADET SERGEANTS
C. S. WALDO, *First Sergeant*   W. T. STERLING, *Supply Sergeant*
H. M. RANDELLS   M. S. WINTER

CADET CORPORALS
C. UHLRICH	E. WILLIAMS	T. S. RATTS
S. WALTON	J. STEINER	G. N. VOWEL

CADET PRIVATES
P. B. PEDRICK	C. B. ROBERTS	H. STURGEON
P. J. PHILLIPS	D. ROBERTS	E. R. SWEET
P. D. PIATT	L. E. ROSSEL	H. I. TARPLEY
C. W. PRATT	G. L. RUCKER	C. L. TURLEY
H. R. PRIESTLY	F. T. RUSSEL	E. F. WAKEFIELD
M. PTACEK	L. J. ST. JOHN	L. WARLICK
R. J. PURVER	M. H. SALISBURY	W. W. WEAVER
C. D. QUIGLEY	D. SCHWARTZ	V. E. WHAN
J. N. RAGLE	R. N. SEARS	L. WHEARTY
E. H. RAYMOND	R. E. SHAFER	J. E. WILLIAMS
T. REAZIN	R. E. SHUART	E. H. WILLIS
G. W. REED	V. SIMONS	R. WOOLNICK
O. B. REED	V. SOLT	H. WORSTER
J. RIDDELL	G. S. SMITH	A. D. ZOOK
	J. S. STEWART	

Company D

CADET CAPTAIN
C. C. McPherson

CADET LIEUTENANTS
W. J. Bucklee, *First Lieutenant*   D. N. Keas, *Second Lieutenant*

CADET SERGEANTS
N. P. Combs, *First Sergeant*   R. G. Frye, *Supply Sergeant*
N. S. Spangler   O. D. Cox

CADET CORPORALS

G. S. Davis	R. S. Jennings	R. N. Neely
R. O. Day	E. R. Kraybill	W. J. Overton

CADET PRIVATES

R. Abbott	R. Guipre	L. V. Morris
V. Bentley	F. Hagens	R. Morrison
N. D. Bruce	P. Hershey	L. R. Mulliken
H. Burgwin	F. R. Hines	H. Orr
J. E. Byer	C. Hogan	L. Riley
L. M. Clark	H. Humburg	W. Robinson
R. S. Coon	H. Humphry	W. Rolfe
J. Cunningham	H. Karns	W. Sartorius
R. E. Early	W. H. Koenig	L. B. Smith
Ray Ewalt	I. Lewis	G. Sutter
V. E. Fletcher	A. Lyon	B. Thompson
C. Glatt	L. N. Marshall	F. W. Williams
R. Gross	E. Means	E. Wintermute
	R. J. Wismer	

ORGANIZATIONS

Y·W·C·A

MISS MILDRED INSKEEP

Wherein lies her power? In her adherence to truth, loyalty to friends, universal kindness and helpfulness, innate refinement, peace and quiet dignity.

𝔜. 𝔚. 𝕮. 𝔄. Reception Room

THE YOUNG WOMEN'S CHRISTIAN ASSOCIATION, founded at Kansas State Agricultural College in 1885, has grown steadily in size and influence until today it stands as the one all-college organization where women can work and serve in the common cause of making Christian citizenship a reality on our college campus. Every girl, regardless of belief or creed, is coming to have a deep interest in the activities of the Christian Association and finds through, service for others, a larger fuller college life. The women of the college by untiring interest and devotion have made this association a power at K. S. A. C. It stands as a monument to their efforts.

Y. W. C. A. Cabinet

Top row—Circle, Gramse, Olmstead, Heiser, Herrick, Cuthbert, Droll
Bottom row—Morris, Thomas, Furneaux, Wilkin, Davis, Mason, Crumbaker, Robertson

OFFICERS

Ruth Thomas	*President*
Elsie Cuthbert	*Vice-President*
Sarella Herrick	*Secretary*
Lucile Heiser	*Treasurer*

COMMITTEE CHAIRMEN

Greeta Gramse	*Social Service*
Mary Crumbaker	*Association News*
Ada Robertson	*Music*
Abbie Furneaux	*Social*
Mary Mason . . .	*Bible Study and Missionary*
Edna Wilkin	*Finance*
Elziabeth Circle . .	*Conferences and Conventions*
Vera Olmstead	*Big Sister*
Mary Frances Davis . . .	*Religious Meetings*
Luella Morris	*Membership*
Mildred Inskeep	*General Secretary*
Hattie Droll	*Student Secretary*

Some of the Girls Who Make the Y. W. C. A. Successful

FIRST CABINET   FRESHMAN COMMISSION

ASSOCIATE CABINET   OCTETTE

SUMMER

AT

HOLLISTER

YWCA
ANNUAL CABINET
HOUSE PARTY

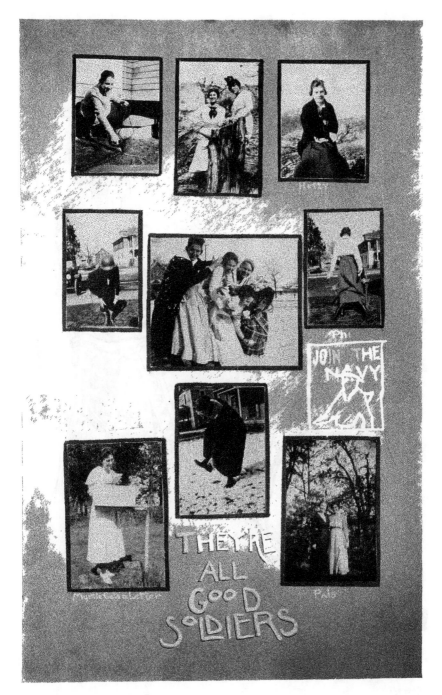

JOIN THE NAVY

THEY'RE ALL GOOD SOLDIERS

LITERARIES

Alpha Beta

Colors—Blue and Gold.   *Motto*—"Slowly but surely we progress."

MEMBERS

Senior

OLIVE LOGERSTROM

Juniors

EVA GWIN
S. W. HONEYWELL
M. J. LUCAS

HOWARD BRAUM

J. O. BROWN
W. I. TURNER
WM. TURNBULL

Sophomores

GRACE TURNER
EVERETT KAIN
BERTHA GWIN

DOROTHY MOSELEY

CHRISTEL ATCHISON
W. I. STERLING
W. O. McCARTH

Freshmen

ALICE MONTGOMERY
WM. LOBAUGH
EMMETT KRAYBILL
TRACY JOHNTZ
PARKS PEDRICK
WALLACE WEAVER
CAROL BUTTON

MILDRED RUST
LAWRENCE BYERS
MABEL WOOSTER
JOHN RUST
RUTH CRAWSON
ARTHUR GRAVES
GEORGE FILLINGER

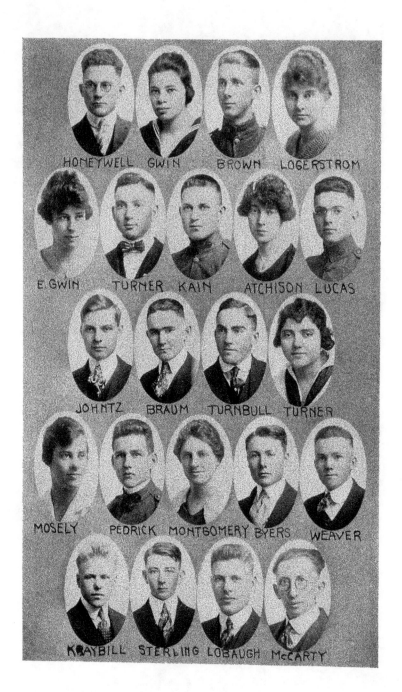

HONEYWELL GWIN BROWN LOGERSTROM

E. GWIN TURNER KAIN ATCHISON LUCAS

JOHNTZ BRAUM TURNBULL TURNER

MOSELY PEDRICK MONTGOMERY BYERS WEAVER

KRAYBILL STERLING LOBAUGH McCARTY

Franklin Literary Society

MEMBERS

Graduates

NELLIE HUNT CONVERSE

MERLE CONVERSE

PERCY DEPUY

Seniors

MARY COVERT
MINNIE DUBBS
NORA MAY DAPPEN

HELEN GOTT
RUTH HUFF
HELEN PETRIE

ARTHUR F. SWANSON
ETHEL SWITZER
NETTIE MAY WISMER

Juniors

THOMAS BAUMGARTEN
ROY CARR

MARY HILL
HARRY MOORE

AMANDA ROSENQUIST
FLOYD WORK

Sophomores

JEANE BAKER
MYRTLE CAREY
ROBERT LUSH

FRANZ J. MASS
FRANCIS NETTLETON

MABLE SWANSON
JOSEPH THACKREY
GERDA OLSON

Freshmen

MARGARET DUBBS
EARLE BURKE

EDITH MUIR

SIDNEY WALTON
CORINNE THIELE

Specials

Bess Curry

S. J. FAIRCHILD

Honor Roll

GLEN ALLEN
JAMES ALSOP
MALCOM ALSOP
THOS. BAUMGARTEN
FRANK BLAIR
JUDSON BLACK
WALTER BURGEN
EVERETT BILLINGS
ROY CARR
GLEN CASE
RAYMOND CAMPBELL
MILLER COE
MERLE CONVERSE
PERCY DEPUY
GLEN EBERWEIN
S. J. FAIRCHILD
G. W. GIVENS
C. S. GOLDSMITH

LEW GRIFFING
A. C. HANCOCK
CHESTER HERRICK
DALTON R. HOOTEN
E. E. HUFF
ORVAN JOSSERAND
LEA JEWETT
JAY LUSH
ROBERT LUSH
FRANZ J. MAAS
ALBERT MACK
ERNEST MILLER
W. S. McCOLLOUGH
T. E. MOORE
ROY MYERS
FRANCIS NETTLETON
R. S. ORR
RALPH RAMSEY

ELLIOT RANNEY
O. W. REED
R. A. SEATON
E. L. SHATTUCK
WM. E. STANLEY
COSH SHELLHAMMER
ARTHUR F. SWANSON
JOE THACKREY
WALLACE THACKREY
MANLEY TINKLER
M. G. TORRENCE
MARK WENTZ
R. T. WILSON
JOE WILLIAMS
CAREY WITHAM
FLOYD WORK
J. W. WORTHINGTON
HOMER RUSSELL

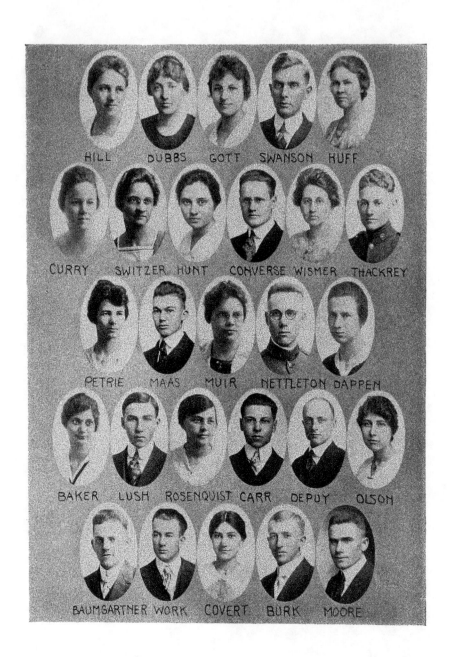

HILL DUBBS GOTT SWANSON HUFF

CURRY SWITZER HUNT CONVERSE WISMER THACKREY

PETRIE MAAS MUIR NETTLETON DAPPEN

BAKER LUSH ROSENQUIST CARR DEPUY OLSON

BAUMGARTNER WORK COVERT BURK MOORE

Ionian Literary Society

Colors—Silver and Gold. *Motto*—Diamond cut diamond.

MEMBERS

Seniors

MIDGE AUSTIN
MILDRED BERRY
RUTH BLAIR
IVYL BARKER
VELMA CARSON
ELIZABETH COTTON
HATTIE GESNER

ESTHER LATZKE
SARA CHASE YOST
HATTIE DROLL
ALPHA LATZKE
HELEN MCILRATH
VERA OLMSTEAD
NELLIE FLO YANTIS

Juniors

DORIS CRANDALL
MARIE HAMMERLY
NELLIE HOARD
ADDA MIDDLETON
ELLA STINSON
DORA CATE
INA FINDLEY
RUTH HARDING

IONE LEITH
ELOISE MORRISON
LEONA TEICHGRAEBER
ELIZABETH CIRCLE
ABBIE FURNEAUX
JESSIE HIBLER
ANNE LORIMER
ANNA ROENIGH

MARGARET WOODMAN

Sophomores

RUBY CANADAY
BLY EWALT
MARGARITE HAMMERLY
DOROTHY POTTER
CLARA SMITH
MARY FRANCES DAVIS
RUTH GILLIS

RUTH HARRISON
ETHEL ROOP
IRENE HOFFINES
MARY DUDLEY
IRENE GRAHAM
LUELLA MORRIS
URSULA SENN

Freshmen

FLORENCE AUSTIN
HESTER HACKNEY
ORPHA MAUST
OLIVETTE MITCH
MARION BROOKOVER

KATHRYN MCQUILLEN
ELSIE PUCKEY
MIRIAM HARLING
GRACE MERRILAT
VERA MCCLELLAND

COTTON OLMSTEAD YOST STINSON GESNER BARKER BERRY CARSON

HOFFHINES CIRCLE MIDDLETON AUSTIN HEIZER CATE BLAIR DROLL

GRAHAM DUDLEY TEICHGRABER EWALT McILRATH FURNEAUX DAVIS CANADY

WEBB HARDING LORIMER ROENIGH FINDLEY A.LATZKE HAMMERLY HAMMERLY

WOODMAN MERRILATT GILLES E.LATZKE HIBLER LEITH ROOP MAUST

HACKNEY YANTIS HARRISON SENN WAUGH McQUILLAN PUCKEY HARLING

MORRIS POTTER BROOKOVER HOARD SMITH AUSTIN McCLELLAND CRANDALL

Hamilton Literary Society

Colors—Red and White   *Motto*—"Truth conquers all."

MEMBERS

Seniors

BARNES, H. D.

BARRINGER, C. M.

CROSS, HOMER

HAMILTON, G. W.

MILLER, G. A.

McCRACKEN, G. W.

PAINTER, J. S.

WILLIAMSON, E. T.

Juniors

FORNEY, W. E.

GRADY, J. F.

HAWKINS, FLOYD

HICKMAN, H. B.

JELDON, J. E.

LYONS, E. S.

McGRATH, L. A.

QUISENBERRY, K. S.

SWINGLE, C. F.

THAYER, D. E.

WILCOX, A. W.

WILLIAMS, J. E.

YOST, T. H.

Sophomores

BINFORD, I. C.

BUSH, G. H.

CIRCLE, R. S.

DePUY, A. C.

GARDNER, O. D.

GILBERT, E. E.

HALL, L. F.

HOWELLS, O. D.

MANGLESDORF, PAUL

McCLELLAND, H. N.

NELSON, O. F.

STEANSON, OSCAR

ST. JOHN, A. P.

Freshmen

CHASE, V. A.

FINDLEY, G. E.

FRANK, K. C.

GATES, G. E.

GILBERT, S. J.

HENNES, F J.

HOWARD, H. E.

MUELLER, E. J.

ROBERTS, C. B.

SELLERS, L. R.

ZOOK, A. D.

GRADY McCRACKEN SWINGLE HAMILTON CROSS

WILCOX LYONS TALLEY MILLER PAINTER YOST

STEANSON MANGLESDORF JELDEN CHASE WILLIAMSON

GILBERT BARNES MAGRATH THAYER WILLIAMS HICKMAN

BARRINGER FORNEY DePUY HOWARD NELSON

HENRY BUSH FINDLEY FRANK CIRCLE McCLELLAN

Browning Literary Society

Colors—Brown and Blue.   *Motto*—"We'll keep our aim sublime."

MEMBERS

Seniors

MILDRED BROWNING
LUCILE CAREY
RUBY ELLERMAN
MYRTLE GUNSELMAN
ETHEL MITCHEL
NELL SHOUP

MARGARET BROWN
QUINTA CATES
EVA HARVEY
VERA SAMUEL
RUTH PHILLIPS
LOLA SLOOP

ALTA HEPLER

Juniors

HETTIE CARRIS
MAY DAHNKE
HELEN DAWLEY
GRACE GISH
CHARLOTTE RUSSELL
JEWELL SAPPENFIELD
ELIZABETH WHETSTONE
MABLE BENTLEY

VERA CATES
VERLA DAHNKE
MARGARET ETZOLD
MAMIE GRIMES
BLANCHE SAPPENFIELD
LUCRETIA SCHOLER
LULU DEIST
ALDA CONROW

Sophomores

GLADYS ADDY
GLADYS CARSON
FLORENCE MATHER
CAROLINE SLOOP

GLADYS BUSHONG
CLARA BELLE HOWARD
ELVA PRICE
MATTIE WASHBURN

LEE WINTER

Freshmen

ELLA FRANZ
BERTHA BURKE
ELSIE FULTON

ADAH SONGER
LUCILE COOPER
BESSIE RUSSELL

GERTRUDE FLOWERS

Orator
MABLE BENTLEY

Debaters

MYRTLE GUNSELMAN
LOLA SLOOP
JEWELL SAPPENFIELD
BLANCHE SAPPENFIELD

MABLE BENTLEY
LUCRETIA SCHOLER
GLADYS ADDY
FLORENCE MATHER

CLARA BELLE HOWARD

L. SLOOP   CAREY   SHOOP   BROWNING   GUMSELMAN   SAMUEL

HOWARD   B. SAPPENFIELD   MITCHELL   DAWLEY   CATES   ETZOLD   V. DAHNKE

BENTLEY   ELLERMAN   M. DAHNKE   PHILLIPS   CARRIS   C. SLOOP

BUSHONG   CONROW   HEPLER   J. SAPPENFIELD   JENNINGS   WHETSTONE   HARVEY

GRIMES   GISH   B. RUSSELL   FRANZ   ADDY   WINTER

CARSON   SCHOLER   WASHBURN   MCINTYRE   C. RUSSELL   MATHER   BROWNE

DIEST   GILBERT   BURKE   HARTLEY   FULTON   PRICE

Athenian Literary Society

Colors—Purple and Old Gold.   *Motto*—"We strive to conquer."

MEMBERS

Seniors

T. Barger
W. W. Bell
F. H. Collins
S. Fairman

C. S. Rude

Fred Griffee
E. M. Hiestand
R. W. Kilbourn
E. J. Price.

Juniors

G. N. Brown
A. N. Burditt
V. S. Crippen
A. B. Collum
M. Duphorne
H. Fairman

C. E. Hutto

R. Hilliard
W. R. Horlacher
L. H. Hoffman
C. J. Medlin
M. P. Schaegel
K. D. Thompson

Sophomores

Nelson Boyle
H. C. Corothers
V. Cool
Oscar Cullen
Ray Knox

R. W. McCall
C. C. McPherson
Lee Parish
A. D. Weber
R. B. Watson

Freshmen

Dale Allen
J. W. Barger
Raymond Bradley
H. P. Bryson
R. Cooper
Earl Domoney
A. Englund

F. A. Swanson

V. Englund
M. A. Graham
C. E. Graves
C. H. Howe
G. H. James
H. E. Mather
E. Sweet

Orator

C. J. Medlin

Debaters

T. Barger
J. W. Barger
A. N. Burditt
A. Englund
S. Fairman
E. Sweet

C. J. Medlin

M. A. Graham
C. E. Graves
W. R. Horlacher
R. W. McCall
E. J. Price
K. D. Thompson

McPHERSON   H. FAIRMAN   GRIFFEE   T. BARGER   RUDE   S. FAIRMAN

HILLIARD   KILBOURNE   THOMPSON   MEDLIN   BELL   KNOX   PRICE

COLLOM   HUTTO   SWEET   BRYSON   COLLINS   CRIPPEN

BOYLE   McCALL   HOFFMAN   J. W. BARBER   BROWN   KORLACHER   SCHLAEGEL

COOL   CULLEN   WATSON   GRAHAM   MATHER   A. ENGLUND

SWANSON   DUPHORNE   HOWE   PARRISH   WEBER   V. ENGLUND   HIGGLAND

ATHENIAN LITERARY SOCIETY

Eurodelphian

Colors—Brown and Gold.   Motto—"While we live, let us live."

MEMBERS

Seniors

Ruth Allen
Ravena Brown
Mary Crumbaker
Margaret Crumbaker
Bertha Flynn
Greeta Gramse
Marie Gehr

Sarella Herrick
Gussie Johnson
Mary Mason
Pearl Miltner
Roccina Parker
Frances Russell
Ruth Thomas

Juniors

Genevra Adams
Ernestine Biby
Mary Gorham
Gladys Ganshird
Dora Grogger
Hazel Howe
Winifred West
Helen Johnson

Elithe Kaull
Bettie Lyman
Irene Miller
Ada Robertson
Laverne Webb
Edna Wilkin
Alma Wilkin
Faye Williams

Sophomores

Minnie Augustine
Charlotte Ayers
Bertha Biltz
Bessie Birkdall
Christine Cool
Marian Clarke
Jessie Evans
Conie Foot

Mable Ginter
Henrietta Jones
Marian Muse
Faye Powell
Dorothy Rhyherd
Gladys Ritts
Marcia Seeber
Helen Sloan

Freshmen

Lillian Ayers
Mary Bird

Elizabeth Dickens
Eva Leland

Ruth Peck

Sponsors

Miss Hunt

Miss Averill

Orator

Gussie Johnson

Debaters

Christine Cool

Gussie Johnson

HOOTS   THOMAS   MASON   BIBY   GRAMSE   HERRICK   FLYNN

CRUMBAKER LYMAN   BILTZ   JOHNSON CRUMBAKER MILLER   PARKER   RUSSELL

WEST   ADAMS   H.JOHNSON   BROWN   MILTNER   GORHAM   ROBERTSON

JONES   SEEBER   WEBB   POWELL   FOOTE   E.WILKINS WILLIAMS   GROGGER

BURKDOLL   CLARKE   KAULL   LELAND   C.AYERS   ALLEN   COOL

EVANS   GANSHIRD A.WILKENS RITTS   MUSE   BIRD   BOELL   HOWE

DICKENS   GINTER   RYHERD   SLOAN   GEHR   L.AYERS AUGUSTINE

Webster Literary Society

Colors—Green and White   *Motto*—"Labor conquers all"

MEMBERS

Seniors

B. B. Brewer   R. D. Nichols

W. T. Foreman

Juniors

E. W. Frost   George Corbet

A. C. Ramsey   C. A. Thresher

Sophomores

J. F. Brown   John Keene

Claire Brown   Walter Law

A. B. Schmidt   Walter Neibarger

Freshmen

Chester Bradshaw   Earl Conrad

Roy Clegg   Earl Means

H. B. Hunt   Walter Rolfe

Erwin Scott   Lawrence Whearty

Philomathian Literary Society

Motto—"Live to learn and learn to live."

Colors—Blue and Gold   Emblem—Marguerite

OFFICERS

First Semester

EMMA STUTZ	President
HAZEL MAY	Vice-President
MARY FRANKHAUSER	Secretary

Second Semester

ETHEL RUTHRUFF	President
IRENE PIERATT	Vice-President
STELLA HARCHEM	Secretary

Lincoln Literary Society

Colors—Navy Blue and Gray   *Motto*—" Knowledge is Golden"

OFFICERS

First Semester

J. R. SMITHHEISLER	*President*
T. B. BETTS	*Vice-President*
. V. BARRINGTON	*Secretary*
R. G. SLOOP	*Treasurer*

Second Semester

H. G. SLOOP	*President*
R. V. BARRINGTON	*Vice-President*
T. B. BETTS	*Secretary*
H. METZ	*Treasurer*

BROWNING

Enjoying Life

Are'nt They Tough?

The War Bride

The Sisters

Industrious

In Forest Dim

Back To The Primitive

The Twain

Baby-bye

Wading

IONIAN

Holding Hands

Lucile Steps Out

Minstrels

Bunched

At To Camp

On The Green

Inseparables

Engineering Association

Pres. H. FAIRMAN, Vice-Pres. H. G. SCHULTZ, Sec. F. WESTCOTT, Treas. E. WILLIAMSON

BRANCHES of two national engineering societies, The American Institute of Electrical Engineers and Mechanical Engineers, have been established at the Kansas State Agricultural College for the benefit of the engineering students. These societies hold bi-weekly meetings, at which papers and discussions based on their experience and study are presented by students and teachers. At frequent intervals practicing engineers from the outside are secured to address the students.

The Architectural Club, composed of students and instructors in architecture, and the Civil Engineers Society, composed of students and instructors in civil engineering, also meet bi-weekly for a purpose similar.

The Engineers' Association is composed of students from all curricula of the division of Engineering. Its objects are to further the interests of the division in the College and the state, and to promote acquaintenceship and fellowship among the students of the division. It meets bi-weekly, the meetings alternating with those of the departmental organizations, and with them constituting the seminar of the Engineering division. Members of the Engineering faculty and eminent consulting engineers present addresses on the engineering topics at these meetings. The Engineers' Association also issues semi-annually "The K. S. A. C. Engineer," a publication dealing with the activities of the engineering division.

STEAM ENGINE LABORATORY

APPLIED MECHANICS LABORATORY

MACHINE SHOPS LABORATORY

ELECTRICAL ENGINEERING LABORATORY

Saddle and Sirloin

Top row—Woodward, Rochford, Nichols, Barringer, Price, Robison, Angle, Whedon
Bottom row—Thompson, Horlacher, Pearson, Howard, Montague, Wise, Morrison,
Willis, Cool.

Colors—Black and Gold

Motto—Better Live Stock for Kansas

The Jayhawker Saddle and Sirloin Club was organized January 17, 1914. The Club is composed of senior, junior and sophomore students in the department of Animal Husbandry in the division of agriculture. The purpose of the organization is to promote the breeding of better live stock in Kansas. A stock judging contest is held every spring in which any student in college may participate.

MEMBERS

C. M. Barringer	N. Pearson
J. H. Cool	E. J. Price
L. M. Howard	W. E. Robinson
W. R. Horlacher	L. H. Rochford
J. D. Montague	E. F. Whedon
R. V. Morrison	H. B. Willis
Phil Neal	H. Wise
R. D. Nichols	H. S. Woodward

Mark Upson

Veterinary Medical Association

Organized October, 1906

The object of this organization is technical training along veterinary lines, together with such social and literary training as may accompany it. Two meetings are held each month and consist of a program and the regular business meeting. The program consists of discussions by the faculty, prominent men in allied lines and the students themselves. Upon graduation all members in good standing are given sheep skins in recognition of their work.

ACTIVE MEMBERS

Seniors

H. J. Austin
A. E. Bate
F. R. Beaudette
J. Erdley
R. F. Coffey
H. A. O'Brien

G. M. Umberger
H. Ikard
F. B. Young
C. E. Zollinger
A. C. Shottenburg
R. P. Parker

C. A. King

Juniors

L. B. Bate
I. F. Gatz
E. S. Bacon
B. F. Taylor
S. L. Hunt
B. L. Erickson
L. V. Skidmore
M. A. MacGrath
W. B. Schlaegel
P. Z. Hixson

J. Stanton
B. B. White
G. M. Simpson
R. Johnson
J. E. Williams
J. Ritter
R. Q. Phipps
I. Thornburg Mock
E. M. Berroth
H. Hicklin

Sophomores

E. Tunnelcliffe
Lee Scott
J. A. Bogue

F. R. Jelden
G. M. Morgan
C. Gallagher

Freshmen

F. Williams
J. A. McKittrick
B. S. Farley

F. L. Simondson
B. Bates
P. X. Cole

ZOLLINGER   HIXON   A.E.BATE   UMBERGER   COFFEY

L.B.BATE   AUSTIN   SCHATTENBERG   IKARD   O'BRIEN

MOCK   JELDEN   TAYLOR   KING   GATZ

SCHLAEGEL   PARKER   McGRATH   HICKMAN   BEAUDETTE

WHITE   F.WILLIAMS   BACON   J.E.WILLIAMS   YOUNG   TUNNICLIFF

Tri=K

Top row—HIESTAND, LYONS, KELLEY, GRIFFEE, SWANSON, BELL
Middle row—RODEWALD, LAUDE, WATERS, McCAMPBELL, YOST
Bottom row—JANSSEN, TRACE, BLAIR, AGNEW

HONORARY AGRONOMY SOCIETY

Colors—Green and Gold   *Flower*—Sunflower

The Klod and Kernel Klub was organized at the Kansas State Agricultural College April 6, 1917. It is composed of faculty, and senior, junior and sophomore students in the agronomy department of the division of agriculture. The purpose of Tri-K is to develop a good feeling between the faculty and students and to promote and advance agronomic activities in this college.

ACTIVE MEMBERS

Faculty

L. E. CALL	M. C. SEWELL	C. C. CUNNINGHAM
S. C. SALMON	J. W. ZAHNLEY	H. J. BOWER
R. I. THROCKMORTON	W. E. GRIMES	G. H. PHINNEY
J. H. PARKER	B. S. WILSON	WILL TUTTLE

Students

W. W. BELL	C. W. McCAMPBELL	BOYD AGNEW
W. C. JANSSEN	E. L. MacINTOSH	CARL TRACE
FRED GRIFFEE	V. S. CRIPPEN	G. L. KELLEY
E. M. HIESTAND	THEODORE YOST	A. N. WATERS
G. Y. BLAIR	W. W. RODEWALD	E. S. LYONS
C. F. LAUDE	A. F. SWANSON	K. S. QUISENBERRY

Prix

Top row—NEIMAN, CATE, GORHAM, STINSON, WILKINS, LORIMER
Bottom row—GUTHRIE, AHRENDS, CIRCLE, ROBERTSON, CARRIS, KAUL

JUNIOR GIRLS' HONOR SOCIETY

MEMBERS

DORA CATE
MARY GORHAM
ELIZABETH CIRCLE
ELITHE KAUL
ADA ROBERTSON
EDNA WILKINS

MILDRED AHRENDS
HELEN NEIMAN
ELLA STINSON
HETTIE CARRIS
IRENE GUTHRIE
ANNE LORIMER

Pep Committee

Top row—DUDLEY, GATZ, HUSTON, HERRICK
Bottom row—WADLEY, CROSS, BOGUE, FOREMAN, CLARK

The Pep Committee which is composed of the president of each class, the editor of the "Collegian," the president of the Y. M. C. A. and the captains of the varsity teams, organizes pep meetings and leads in the support of college athletics.

MEMBERS

SARELLA HERRICK, President Senior Class
IKE GATZ, President Junior Class
MARY DUDLEY, President Sophomore Class
DEWEY HUSTON, President Freshman Class
ELIZABETH WADLEY, Editor "Collegian"
HOMER CROSS, President Y. M. C. A.
J. R. BOGUE, Captain Football Team
W. T. FOREMAN, Captain Track Team
JOHN CLARKE, Captain Basket Ball

Student Council

Top row—BLAIR, KNISELEY, HEISER, SAMUELS, O'BRIEN
Bottom row—GRAHAM, ROSS, ROBERTSON, WILLIS, CARRIS

MEMBERS AND OFFICERS OF STUDENT COUNCIL

Seniors

HOWARD O'BRIEN   LUCILLE HEISER
RUTH BLAIR   VERA SAMUEL

Juniors

HETTIE CARRIS   CLIFFORD KNISELEY
                ADA ROBERTSON

Sophomores

GLADYS ROSS   IRENE GRAHAM

Freshmen
EVERETT WILLIS

OFFICERS

President . . . . . . H. A. O'BRIEN
Vice-President . . . . . HETTIE CARRIS
Secretary . . . . . . VERA SAMUELS

Bethany Circle

Top row—Dudley, Dooley, Dubbs, Vandivert, Stinson, Owens, Samuels, Blaine
Middle row—Willis, Allen, Smith, Reinhardt, Murray, Rudy, Baker
Bottom row—Adams, Grover, Ross, Hamilton, Fleming, Harvey, Flanders, Purdey

Beta Chapter

Founded at Illinois University, 1912.
Installed November 26, 1913.

Colors—Green and White.   *Flower*—Daisy.

Publication—"The Radius."

MEMBERS

Seniors

Vera Samuels
Auroline Vandervert
Eva Harvey

Avis Blain

Minnie Dubbs
Ruth Allen
Mollie Moser

Juniors

Eloise Flanders
Barbara Murray

Mabel Adams
Ella Stinson

Sophomores

Clara Smith
Exene Owens
Abbie Claire Dennon
Caroline Seitz

Mary Dudley
Ruth Willis
Gladys Ford
Pearl Hoots

Freshmen

Hester Ross
Garnet Grover

Margaret Dubbs
Emma Stutz

In Urbe

Grace Rudy
Julia King
Mabel Fleming
Maude Hamilton

Mabel Purdy
Ruth Moore
Orliana Baker
Pearl Dooley

Hazel Campbell

Young Men's Christian Association

Faculty Advisory Committee:

H. L. KENT, Chairman
H. L. DURHAM
J. R. McARTHUR
C. O. SWANSON
L. A. FITZ, Treasurer

Officers:

HOMER CROSS, Student President
W. W. McLEAN, Secretary
C. F. COOL, Substitute Secretary
J. F. DANIELS, War Work Secretary

During the past year the local Young Men's Christian Association has passed through a series of experiences that have brought about a change in the character of its work. In June, the former secretary, Mr. W. W. McLean, sailed for France in the war work service. Upon the establishment of the S. A. T. C. in October, the student cabinet ceased to exist, the Y. M. C. A. building was converted into a barracks, and a reading and lounging room was established on the campus in F3. To further serve the men of the S. A. T. C. the War Work Council provided a hut close by the campus barracks and placed a secretary in charge.

Upon the demobilization of the S. A. T. C., it became necessary for the local Association to re-establish itself. In answer to the general feeling that the organization had not in the past met the existing needs of our student life, it was determined to place the Association upon a broader basis. To that end, a three-fold policy was adopted. The building on the corner of Eleventh and Fremont will be used only for dormitory purposes until such time as it may be disposed of to advantage. The Association headquarters will be located permanently on the campus. A secretary, a man who knows present day college student life, will be secured at a very substantial increase of salary.

The Association looks forward to future growth and development that it may fill its place in the life of K. S. A. C.

Women's Athletic Association

HAMMERLI DANKE   BOND   LORING   WEBB HEISER
GROGGER BILTZ   WILSON BURGER

The Women's Athletic Association was organized in the fall of 1915 for the purpose of promoting the physical and social activities of the women at the Kansas State Agricultural College.

OFFICERS

LUCILE HEISER, President
LOVERNE WEBB, Vice-President
MARIE HAMMERLI, Secretary
VERLA DANKE, Treasurer
BERTHA BILTZ, Hockey Manager
DORA GROGGER, Swimming
GLADYS BURGER, Basket Ball Manager
VERLE DANKE, Tennis Manager
EDITH WILSON, Hike Manager

K Fraternity

Top row—BOGUE, HUSTON, MAGRATH, H. FAIRMAN
Second row—GALLAGHER, L. MILLER, FOLTZ, FROST, HIXON
Third row—GATZ, CLARK, YOUNG, GINGERY, BECKETT, FOREMAN
Bottom row—RODA, WINTERS, RANDALL, KECKER, BURTON

The K fraternity is composed of athletes who have won letters in Aggie athletics.

MEMBERS

J. A. BOGUE
DEWEY HUSTON
L. W. MILLER
L. A. MAGRATH
HOBART FAIRMAN
J. A. CLARK
W. T. FOREMAN
EARL FROST
H. H. RANDALL
E. F. WHEDON

I. F. GATZ
C. O. RODA
M. S. WINTERS
K. H. KECKER
H. BURTON
C. E. BECKETT
CLIFF GALLAGHER
H. GINGERY
G. A. FOLTZ
R. W. HIXON

Purple Masque

Top row—BIBY, HAMILTON, GRAMSE, ROCHFORD
Bottom row—LYMAN, WORKS, CARSON, ENNS, NELSON

The Purple Masque, honorary dramatic fraternity, is composed of persons elected to membership for creditable dramatic work done in the production of a college play.

MEMBERS

ERNESTINE BIBY
LLOYD HAMILTON
GREETA GRAMSE
LOUIS ROCHFORD

BETTY LYMAN
FLOYD WORKS
VELMA CARSON
HENRY ENNS

OLIVER NELSON

Quill Club

Top row—DAVIS, BARKER, MEDLIN, PADDLEFORD, CARSON, CRAWFORD
Middle row—RICE, ANGLE, BENTLEY, POLSON, SHINGLEDECKER, SULLIVAN, MOORE
Bottom row—OAKES, ROWLES, RUSSELL, KLOTZ, McCAMPBELL, BOELL

Colors—Black and White

Flower—Pansy

The Quill Club is an organization composed of persons who have distinguished themselves in literary fields.

MEMBERS

H. W. DAVIS
ADA RICE
N. A. CRAWFORD
IVYL BARKER
CALVIN MEDLIN
IZIL POLSON
MABELL BENTLEY
F. E. OAKS

CLEMENTINE PADDLEFORD
H. A. MOORE
SARAH BOELL
J. B. ANGLE
VELMA CARSON
CHARLOTTE RUSSELL
FLORENCE ROWLES
BERNICE KLOTZ

LAURA SHINGLEDECKER

Forum

An Honorary Society for Debaters and Orators

Motto—"To be, rather than to seem."

"The forum owl sat on an oak,
The more he saw the less he spoke;
The less he spoke the more he heard,
Let's strive to be like that old bird."

THE ROLL

Gladys Addy	Gordon Hamilton	Lee M. Parrish
Christel Atchison	Marguerite Hammerly	Everett Price
Turner Barger, K	Lucille Heiser	Ada Robertson
Wheeler Barger	Mary Hill	Jewell Sappenfield, K
Mabel Bentley	Clara Howard	Blanch Sappenfield, KK
Lindley C. Binford	Walter Horlacher	Lucretia Scholer
Ruth Blair	Floyd Hawkins, KKKKK	Nell Shoup
Jamie Cameron	Gussie Johnson, K	Lola Sloop, KKK
Dora Cates, K	M. J. Lucas	Ella Stinson
Elizabeth Circle, K	Olive Logerstrom, K	Eugene R. Sweet
Christine Cool, K	Florence Mather, K	A. F. Swanson, KK
Elizabeth Cotton	Hilery E. Mather	J. E. Thackery
Mary Dudley	Chas. C. McPherson	K. D. Thompson, K
Arnold Englund	C. J. Medlin, KKK	Grace Turner
Seibert Fairman, K	Helen Mitchell, KK	Lelia Whearty
Samuel Gilbert	H. A. Moore, KKK	Everett H. Willis
Chester E. Graves	Dorothy Moseley, K	Oscar Steanson, K
Irene Graham	Oliver Nelson	R. W. McCall
Marion Graham	Clementine Paddleford	Myrtle Gunselman, K

HONORARY MEMBERS

J. W. Searson

O. H. Burns

Grace Derby

Dr. J. R. Macarthur

DEBATE SCHOLARS

Calvin J. Medlin

Lola Sloop

SLOOP COTTON HAMILTON McARTHUR BLAIR FAIRMAN T.BARGER

SWANSON LOGERSTROM HEISER MEDLIN JOHNSON SHOUP NELSON

McPHERSON CATE PRICE MITCHELL CIRCLE LUCAS GUNSELMAN

J.SAPPENFIELD DUDLEY WHEARTY THOMPSON B.SAPPENFIELD CAMERON FROST

DERBY PADDLEFORD HOWARD NETTLETON STINSON HORLACHER ROBERTSON

GRAHAM SWEET HAMMERLY J.BARGER BENTLEY WILLIS COOL

MOSELEY THACKREY ENGLUND ATCHISON GILBERT HILL STEANSON TURNER

MATHER McCALL ADDY BINFORD W.HEARTY M.GRAHAM MATHER MOORE

©ratorical Board

The Oratorical Board conducts all oratorical contests, making all arrangements and attending to all business concerning it.

The members of the Oratorical Board are:

Eurodelphians
RUTH THOMAS
EDNA WILKINS

Ionians
VELMA CARSON
MARIE HAMMERLY

Websters
THORNTON FOREMAN
EARLE W. FROST

Hamiltons
HOMER CROSS
A. W. WILCOX

Brownings
MAMIE GRIMES
VERA SAMUEL

Franklins
HELEN GOTT
FRANCES NETTLETON

Athenians
SEIBERT FAIRMAN
K. D. THOMPSON

Alpha Betas
OLIVE LOGERSTROM
W. I. TURNER

XIX

Top row—OLMSTEAD, TAYLOR, SLOOP, COTTON, HERRICK, CARSON
Middle row—KRAMER, WEBB, BLAIR, HEISER, THOMAS, BONDURANT, HALLECK
Bottom row—CRUMBAKER, MASON, JOHNSON, GRAMSE, SAMUELS, DROLL

SENIOR HONOR SOCIETY

THE ROLL

VERA OLMSTEAD
LOLA SLOOP
SARELLA HERRICK
EVALENE KRAMER
MARTHA WEBB
RUTH BLAIR
LUCILE HEISER
RUTH THOMAS
FAYNE BONDURANT

MARY CRUMBAKER
MARY MASON
GUSSIE JOHNSON
GREETA GRAMSE
VERA SAMUELS
HATTIE DROLL
HAZEL TAYLOR
ELIZABETH COTTON
VELMA CARSON

LUCILE HALLECK

Scarab

SENIOR HONOR SOCIETY

Top row—MYERS, BLAIR, BATE, UMBERGER
Middle row—CLARKE, HAMILTON, BREWER, WHEDON, O'BRIEN
Bottom row—MACGREGOR, BARRINGER, H. FAIRMAN, S. FAIRMAN

THE BEST OF THE CLASS OF '19

CARROLL M. BARRINGER   BRUCE B. BREWER
SEIBERT FAIRMAN   C. H. MYERS
EDWIN F. WHEDON   JOHN A. CLARKE
GAIL UMBERGER   R. D. MACGREGOR
GEORGE Y. BLAIR   GORDON W. HAMILTON
HOWARD A. O'BRIEN   HOBART FAIRMAN

ARTHUR E. BATE

Sororities

Pi Beta Phi

Top row—BIBY, DAWSON, GILES, BLANK, WEBB, ADAMS, HERRICK
Middle row—BRETCH, GUTHRIE, BIGGS, MILLER, FORSYTHE, TROUTFETTER, KINMAN, MOORE
Bottom row—ANDREWS, EPPLER, HANNA, HAYNES, CATON, ROARK, EPPERSON

Founded at Monmouth College, 1867; Kansas Beta Chapter, 1915.

Colors—Wine and Silver Blue. *Flower*—Wine Carnation.

Publication—"The Arrow."

MEMBERS

Seniors

EDITH BIGGS	MARTHA WEBB	ELIZABETH ADAMS
HELEN BLANK	LOUISE DAWSON	RUTH MOORE
SARELLA HERRICK		

Juniors

ERNESTINE BIBY	RUTH EPPLER	MABEL TROUTFETTER
IRENE MOTT GUTHRIE	LOIS HANNA	MARIE HAYNES

Sophomores

ESTHER ANDREWS		WILMIA ROARK
HELEN GILES	MARION BRETCH	KATHERIN KINMAN

Freshmen

GOODNER FORSYTHE	HORTENSE CATON	MARGUERITE MILLER

Pledges

HELEN THAYER	JESSIE HIBLER	MARGARET EPPERSON

Delta Delta Delta

Top row—Barker, Burgner, Neiman, Halleck, Haack, Beggs, Seeds, Conroy
Middle row—Woodward, Sterling, Turner, Bauerfield, Burris, Boon, Glenn
Bottom row—Varner, Calkins, Young, Tegmeire, Willis, Heath, Potter, Fisher

Founded at Boston University, 1888.   Kansas Iota Chapter.
Colors—Silver, Gold and Blue.   *Flower*—Pansy.
Publication—"The Trident."

MEMBERS
Seniors

Mary Haack		Lucile Halleck
Adelaide Seeds		Ivyl Barker

Juniors

Fay Young		Elizabeth Burger
Elizabeth Glenn		Gladys Woodward
	Helen Neiman	

Sophomores

Mildred Sterling	Gertrude Conroy	Ruth Willis
Dorothy Potter	Helen Calkins	Fanny Belle Beggs

Freshmen

Winifred Varner	Elizabeth Heath	Rowena Turner
Marjorie Fisher	Marie Burris	Alma Bauersfield
	Burdette Tegmeire	

Special
Elizabeth Boon

Sorores in Facultate
Miss Joy Andrews   Miss Martha Denny

Sorores in Urbe

Mrs. E. N. Wentworth		Mrs. Theodore Macklin
Mrs. A. M. Patterson	Mrs. Arthur Fielding	Miss Hazel Mason

Chi Omega

Top row—BONDURANT, CURRY, TAYLOR, F. MITCHELL, STANLEY, R. CROCKER, BURTON, RICE
Middle row—RALSTON, ROBINSON, A. CROCKER, BONDURANT, PETERSON, FORD, HALL
Bottom row—CHAMPION, NEAL, KIRKPATRICK, SHUMAKER, A. MITCHELL, HALSEY, MILLER, BROWN

Founded at Fayetteville, Arkansas, 1895. Installed 1915.
Colors—Cardinal and Straw. *Flower*—White Carnation.
Publication—"The Eleusis."

MEMBERS

Seniors

RUTH TAYLOR
MARY KIRKPATRICK

FAYNE BONDURANT

LOIS BURTON
BESS CURRY

Juniors

ALICE RICE

RUBY CROCKER

PRUDENCE STANLEY

Sophomores

JOSEPHINE SHUMAKER
ANNA MARIE CROCKER

EDITH RALSTON
NELL ROBINSON

Freshmen

ENOLA MILLER
ALICE MITCHELL

MARGUERITE BONDURANT
ARRIA NEAL

Pledges

GLADYS PETERSON
ELSA BROWN

HELEN HALSEY
MILDRED CHAMPION

Delta Zeta

Top row—KRAMER, EDGERTON, HOAG, WILSON, WAKEFIELD, HOAG, GLEASON
Middle row—O. KLOTZ, P. PARKHURST, ROOP, MURRAY, POLSON, R. PARKHURST, GROVER, B. KLOTZ
Bottom row—DUBBS, LOCKE, WEST, ROBERTSON, MCINTYRE, BRAINERD, CLARKE

Founded at Miami University, Oxford, Ohio, 1902. Lambda Chapter Installed 1915.

Colors—Old Rose and Nile Green. *Flower*—Pink Rose.

Publication—"The Lamp."

MEMBERS

Seniors

LENORE EDGERTON	EDYTHE WILSON	EVELYN KRAMER

Juniors

EDITH WAKEFIELD	BARBARA MURRAY	WINIFRED WEST
LEAH MCINTYRE	RUBY PARKHURST	ADA ROBERTSON
	PEARL PARKHURST	

Sophomores

LYLE HOAG	BERNICE KLOTZ	VIOLA BRAINERD
DOROTHY GLEASON	ETHEL ROOP	OLLIE KLOTZ
	MARIAN CLARKE	

Freshmen

GARNET GROVER	MADELINE LOCKE	NETTIE DUBBS

In Urbe

IZIL POLSON   LEONA HOAG

Alpha Delta Pi

Top row—UHLEY, BORTHWICK, GRAMSE, ARENDS, GANN, SULLIVAN, TAYLOR
Middle row—GLENN, PADDLEFORD, BACHMAN, STEWART, GARVIN, KAULL, CAMERON, MESERVE
Bottom row—LAMBERTSON, D. BACHMAN, BURGESS, BROWN, LAWRENCE, WISHARD, LOVETT

Founded at Weslyan Female College, Macon, Georgia, 1851.
Alpha Eta Chapter Installed 1915.

Colors—Blue and White.   Flower—Violet.

Publication—"Adelphian."

MEMBERS

Seniors

MURL GANN   HAZEL TAYLOR
GERTRUDE UHLEY   RUTH BORTHWICK   GREETA GRAMSE

Juniors

OPAL WISHARD   FRANCES LOVETT
INEZ BACHMAN .   HELEN LAWRENCE   VELMA MESERVE
JOSEPHINE SULLIVAN   MILDRED AHRENDS   ELITHE KAULL

Sophomores

JAMIE CAMERON   LILLIAN STEWART
CLEMENTINE PADDLEFORD   RUTH GARVIN

Freshmen

EVELYN GLENN   ELIZABETH BROWN   ADELIA BACHMAN

Pledges

RUTH LAMBERTON   NINA BURGESS

Sorore in Facultate
MRS. ALICE DOSEY

Kappa Kappa Gamma

Top row—BURT, COTTON, GOODRUM, CORBY, M. MERILLAT, ROSS, GORHAM, RITTER
Middle row—DUDLEY, WESTCOTT, HAMILTON, DAVIS, JULIAN, LUTZ, TEICHGRAEBER
Bottom row—MERILLAT, DUFF, REINER, DRAKE, SEERY, WEDDLE, HONEYWELL, DALTON

Founded at Monmouth College, 1870.   Gamma Alpha Chapter Installed 1916.

Colors—Light and Dark Blue.   Flower—Fleur de Lis.

Publication—"The Key."

MEMBERS

Seniors

ELIZABETH COTTON
LEONA TEICHGRAEBER

PHYLLIS BURT

NADIA DUNN CORBY
HAZEL MERILLAT WILLIAMS

Juniors

RUTH GOODRUM
MARIE JULIAN

BETTY HART RITTER

MARY GORHAM
VINNIE DRAKE

Sophomores

MARVEL MERILLAT
GLADYS ROSS
IZABEL HAMILTON

NORINE WEDDLE

FRANCES WESTCOTT
ALFREDA HONEYWELL
FLORENCE REINER

Freshmen

ADELAIDE LUTZ
LEAH BELL DUFF

GRACE MERILLAT
IRENE SEERY

Pledges

MARY FRANCES DAVIS   MARY DUDLEY

Josephine

Blue Monday

KKΓ

Ready for Flying

Home Sweet Home

Pledges

Mary

Women's Pan=Hellenic Council

Top row—WOODWARD, BRAINERD, TAYLOR, WEBB, COTTON, SULLIVAN
Bottom row—BONDURANT, DAWSON, WILSON, YOUNG, GANN, TEICHGRAEBER

MEMBERS

Delta Zeta
> VIOLA BRAINERD
> EVALENE KRAMER

Kappa Kappa Gamma
> ELIZABETH COTTON
> LEONA TEICHGRAEBER

Chi Omega
> RUTH TAYLOR
> FAYNE BONDURANT

Pi Beta Phi
> LOUISE DAWSON
> MARTHA WEBB

Alpha Delta Pi
> JOSEPHINE SULLIVAN
> MURL GANN

Delta Delta Delta
> GLADYS WOODWARD
> FAY YOUNG

Freshmen Girls' Pan=Hellenic Council

Top row—GLENN, BONDURANT, DAVIS, MILLER, FISHER, KLOTZ
Bottom row—HANNA, LOCKE, LAMBERTSON, PETERSON, TURNER, HONEYWELL

The Freshmen Girls' Pan Hellenic Council was organized for the purpose of promoting good fellowship as well as co-operating with the Senior Pan Hellenic in matters of fraternity interest.

MEMBERS

Pi Beta Phi
    LOIS HANNA
    MARGUERITE MILLER

Delta Zeta
    MADELINE LOCKE
    BERNICE KLOTZ

Delta Delta Delta
    MARJORIE FISHER
    ROWENA TURNER

Kappa Kappa Gamma
    MARY FRANCES DAVIS
    ALFREDA HONEYWELL

Alpha Delta Pi
    EVELYN GLENN
    RUTH LAMBERTSON

Chi Omega
    GLADYS PETERSON
    MARGUERITE BONDURANT

Enchiladas

Top row—KRAMER, WEBB, BONDURANT, HALLECK, GANN, TEICHGRAEBER
Bottom row—BIBY, BURT, BACHMAN, McINTYRE, SEEDS, RICE

Chi Omega
    RUBY CROCKER
    ALICE RICE
    EDITH HALL
    NELL ROBINSON
    PRUDENCE STANLEY
    FAYNE BONDURANT

Pi Beta Phi
    IRENE MOTT GUTHRIE
    ERNESTINE BIBY
    LOUISE DAWSON
    MABLE TROUTFETTER
    HELEN BLANK
    MARTHA WEBB

Delta Delta Delta
    GERTRUDE CONROY
    GLADYS WOODWARD
    LUCILE HALLECK
    FANNY BELL BEGGS
    FAY YOUNG
    ADELAIDE SEEDS

Delta Zeta
    LEAH McINTYRE
    LENORE EDGERTON
    EVALENE KRAMER
    VIOLA BRAINERD
    DOROTHY GLEASON
    WINIFRED WEST

Kappa Kappa Gamma
    PHYLLIS BURT
    LEONA TEICHGRAEBER
    MARIE JULIAN
    RUTH GOODRUM
    FRANCES WESTCOTT
    MARVEL MERILLAT

Alpha Delta Pi
    INEZ BACHMAN
    VELMA MESERVE
    JOSEPHINE SULLIVAN
    MILDRED AHRENDS
    GERTRUDE UHLEY
    MURL GANN

FRATS

Shamrocks

Organized March 1, 1917

Publication—"Shamrock Leaf"

Colors—Green and White.   *Flower*—Rose of Killarney.

MEMBERS
Seniors

Floyd M. Pickerell   Ralph S. Westcott
Howard A. Lindsley   Mark F. Upson

Homer Willis

Juniors

Lawrence E. Stonge   Warren E. Rothweiler
Lloyd D. Zimmerman   Garnett W. Reed

Sophomores

Ralph E. Lang   Dorsey Denniston
Charles H. Cloud   Hobart I. May
Clare Shellenberger   Harry E. Newton

Earl B. Slason

Freshmen

Harold B. Combs   Lyle D. Leach
George S. Davis   Allen E. Green
Everett Willis   Donald E. Blocksome

Pledges

Dan O. Gordon   Dale Swartz

In Facultate

Armin M. Doerner   Wm. Pickett

Top row—UPSON, ZIMMERSON, SLASON, MAY, STONGE
Second row—WESTCOTT, LEACH, SHELLENBERGER, PICKRELL, GORDON, LINDSEY
Third row—H. WILLIS, REED, ROTWEILER, SWARTZ, COMBS, CLOUD, GREEN
Bottom row—DENNISTON, NEWTON, BLOCKSTONE, E. WILLIS, DAVIS, LANG

Beta Theta Pi

Founded at Miami University, Oxford, Ohio, 1839

Gamma Epsilon Chapter

Installed October 17, 1914

Colors—Pink and Blue   *Flower*—Red Rose

MEMBERS

Seniors

R. A. VAN TRINE   L. B. PTACEK

L. V. RITTER   C. H. MYERS

Juniors

I. F. GATZ   L. R. RITTER

H. T. ENNS, JR.   G. M. SIMPSON

Sophomores

C. N. SMITH   W. C. ROBINSON

D. D. MURPHY   G. S. SMITH

Freshmen

M. E. PTACEK   E. R. ENNS

S. A. SIMPSON   R. V. GROSS

J. C. RIDDELL   J. E. HAAG

O. D. COX   L. B. SMITH

C. L. TURLEY   N. D. BRUCE

FRATRES IN FACULTATE

W. M. JARDINE   C. W. McCAMPBELL

J. D. WALTERS   J. B. GINGERY

H. H. KING   A. M. PATERSON

S. A. SMITH   J. R. GLEISNER

Top row—MURPHY, L. PTACEK, GATZ, L. SMITH, G. SMITH, ROBISON
Second row—MYERS, L. RITTER, GROSS, H. ENNS, G. SIMPSON
Third row—HAAG; BRUCE, TURLEY, M. PTACEK, C. SMITH, S. SIMPSON
Bottom row—L. R. RITTER, E. ENNS, COX, RIDDELL, VAN TRINE

Sigma Alpha Epsilon

Kansas Beta Chapter

Installed January 25, 1913.

Publications—"Record and Phi Alpha."

Founded at University of Alabama, Tuscaloosa, March 9, 1856.

Colors—Purple and Gold.   *Flower*—Violet.

MEMBERS

Seniors

JAY L. WOODHOUSE   LOUIS H. ROCHFORD
JOSEPH H. COOL   CARL V. MALONEY
EVAN H. RICHARDSON

Juniors

HAROLD R. GUILBERT   FRED W. BOYD
JAMES C. SNAPP   DEWEY Z. McCORMICK
JOSEPH N. SAWTELL   CHARLES E. NICHOLS

Sophomores

LAWRENCE E. GRIFFITH   PAUL TUPPER
FLOYD F. COLE   JOHN W. CORDTS
ARTHUR L. MESERVE

Freshmen

ROGER O. DAY   CHARLES S. WALDO
CHARLES E. CORDTS   JAMES B. QUINLAN
G. ROBERT ALLINGHAM

Pledge

HAROLD A. LAYTON

Fratres in Facultate

JOHN R. McCLUNG   FRED W. GREELEY

Sigma Alpha Epsilon

Top row—GRIFFITH, COOL, MESERVE
Second row—MOORE, ALLINGHAM, GUILBERT, SNAPP, TUPPER
Third row—SAWTELL, QUINLAN, DAY, ROCHFORD, NICHOLS, RICHARDSON
Bottom row—WALDO, McCORMICK, LAYTON, COLE, CORDTS

Sigma Nu

Founded at Virginia Military Institute, 1869

Beta Kappa Chapter

Installed May, 1913

Publication—"Delta"

Flower—White Rose.   *Colors*—Black, White and Gold.

MEMBERS

Seniors

B. B. BREWER   CARROL BARRINGER

HOWARD O'BRIEN

Juniors

LLOYD MILLER   CARL MILLER
W. E. ROBISON   W. B. CAREY

Sophomores

R. A. MAUPIN   J. H. EPPERSON
BEN SCHEMONSKI   L. L. HAMILTON
T. J. NEELY   J. P. FALLIS

H. A. GUMNESS

Freshmen

FRED MILLER   C. E. BLECKLEY
F. F. RUSSELL   GAIL LYNCH

Pledges

RAY PLYLEY   S. J. COE

Fratres in Urbe

NAT BLAKE   R. J. HANNA

E. A. WRIGHT

Fratres in Facultate

C. F. BAKER   A. E. WESTBROOK
W. A. LIPPINCOTT   M. C. SEWELL

H. H. HAYMAKER

Sigma Nu

Top row—LYNCH, FALLIS, NEELEY, F. MILLER, MAUPIN, RUSSELL, SCHEMONSKI
Middle row—BARRINGER, PLYLEY, GUNNESS, BLECKLEY, BURTON, O'BRIEN, BREWER
Bottom row—EPPERSON, CAREY, COE, C. MILLER, HAMILTON, ROBISON

Sigma Phi Delta

Organized May 16, 1914.

Colors—Sky Blue and Dark Blue.   *Flower*—Red Carnation.

MEMBERS

Seniors

F. R. Beaudette
A. E. Bate

H. S. Wise

G. W. Hamilton
F. Totten

Juniors

L. B. Bate
E. S. Bacon
F. L. Hall

S. L. Hunt
I. T. Mock
T. Swenson

Sophomore

H. D. Phillips

Freshmen

E. F. Bailey

C. W. Pratt

W. H. Burgwin

Pledges

W. J. Bucklee
W. Sartorius

H. N. Hudson
A. J. Walker

Frater in Facultate

Hugh Durham

Top row—HAMILTON, HALL, TOTTEN, MOCK
Second row—PRATT, BURGWIN, HUNT, L. B. BATE, BAILEY
Third row—BACON, HUDSON, BEAUDETTE, PHILLIPS, WISE
Bottom row—SARTORIUS, SWENSON, BUCKLEE, E. A. BATE

Alpha Psi

Eta Chapter

Founded at Ohio State University January, 1917

Installed April 5, 1912

Colors—Blue and Gold   *Flower*—Red Carnation

MEMBERS

Seniors

A. E. BATE

E. H. IKARD

H. A. O'BRIEN

E. H. RICHARDSON

G. M. UMBERGER

G. M. YOUNG

C. E. ZOLLINGER

Juniors

L. B. BATE

E. M. BERROTH

R. W. HIXON

C. GALLAGHER

I. F. GATZ

Sophomores

J. A. BOGUE

L. G. MORGAN

L. A. SCOTT

E. A. TUNNICLIFF

Pledges

L. A. MAGRATH

J. A. McKITTERICK

M. P. SCHLAEGEL

F. WILLIAMS

B. B. WHITE

In Facultate

DR. R. R. DYKSTRA, D. V. M.

DR. J. H. BURT, D. V. M.

DR. J. B. GINGERY, D. V. M.

E. N. WENTWORTH

DR. N. D. HARWOOD, D. V. M.

DR. C. B. GRIFFITHS, D. V. M.

DR. L. R. VAWTER, D. V. M.

C. W. McCAMPBELL, B. S. A.; M. S. A.

Alpha Psi

Top row—BOGUE, MAGRATH
Second row—LUNNICLIFF, SCOTT, BATES, UMBERGER, HIXON
Third row—GATZ, MORGAN, IKARD, YOUNG, O'BRIEN, ZOLLINGER
Bottom row—GALLAGHER, WILLIAMS, McKITTARCK, E. BATES, BERROTH

Aztex

Organized February 19, 1910.

Publication—"The Arrow."

Colors—Lavender and Blue.   *Flower*—Violet.

MEMBERS

Seniors

GEORGE V. BLAIR   JOHN A. CLARKE
PHILLIP E. NEALE   EDWIN F. WHEDON

Juniors

WALTER GARDNER   CLARENCE L. BROWNING
HENRY G. GENTRY   CLARK O. WORKS
EVERETT COWELL   GEORGE W. HINDS
MARION HOWARD   FRANCIS WELCH

Sophomores

JOHN A. EVANS   HAROLD HOOTS
GEORGE JENNINGS   SHERIDAN S. SPANGLER

RAY E. KELLOG

Freshmen

SCOTT STEWART   DEWEY HOUSTON
WARREN COWELL   GEORGE MORRIS
JAMES ALBRIGHT   LEO CLARK

FABRIQUE CHRISTMAN

In Facultate

L. E. CALL   J. V. CORTELYOU

A. E. McCLYMONDS

Aztex

Top row—HUSTON, SPANGLER, JENNINGS
Second row—ALBRIGHT, EVANS, STEWART, E. COWELL, NEALE, BROWNING
Third row—BLAIR, CHRISTMAN, GARDNER, GENTRY, HOWARD, W. COWELL, KELLOG
Bottom row—MORRIS, HOOTS, CLARKE, HINDS, WHEDON, CLARKE

Sigma Phi Epsilon

Founded at Richmond College, Richmond, Virginia, November 1, 1901.

Kansas Beta Chapter

Installed February 23, 1918

Publication—"Sigma Phi Epsilon Journal."

Colors—Purple and Red.   *Flowers*—American Beauties and Violets.

MEMBERS

Seniors

SEIBERT FAIRMAN

ORIN W. HINSHAW

WILLIAM C. JANSSEN

R. DONALD MACGREGOR

Juniors

CLYDE E. BECKETT

BERNARD B. BROOKOVER

GEORGE M. DRUMM

HOBART FAIRMAN

PAUL L. FETZER

KURT H. KECKER

CLIFFORD KNISELEY

CLAY F. LAUDE

CARL O. RODA

Sophomores

EARL G. ABBOTT

HOLMAN L. BUNGER

REX D. BUSHONG

CHARLES M. HAUGHTON

C. WILLIAM HOWE

RAYMOND C. NICHOLS

CLAUDE B. OWEN

ROBERT B. PIATT

EVERETTE D. STEWART

ROSS W. STICE

M. S. WINTER

Freshmen

CLAUDE O. BECKETT

JACK HILL

CARL G. MCCASLIN

PHIL D. PIATT

E. HERBERT RAYMOND

MORSE H. SALISBURY

R. MAURICE SEARS

ARTHUR J. WILLIAMSON

Pledges

ROGER L. ABBOTT

HAROLD MCGINLEY

In Facultate

JOHN R. MACARTHUR

O. E. REED

Sigma Phi Epsilon

Top row—STICE, KECKLER, C. BECKETT, WINTER, MACGREGOR, HINSHAW, E. ABBOTT
Second row—OWEN, SALISBURY, WILLIAMSON, KNISELEY, HOWE, HILL, P. PIATT
Third row—RODA, JANSSEN, SEARS, MCCASLIN, LAUDE, HOUGHTON, BUNGER, BUSHONG
Bottom row—C. E. BECKETT, S. FAIRMAN, RAYMOND, BROOKOVER, FETZER, R. ABBOTT,
       R. PIATT

Alpha Theta Chi

Organized April 9, 1912

Flower—Wine Rose.   *Colors*—Wine and White.

MEMBERS

Senior

JAMES B. ANGLE

Juniors

W. W. RODEWALD   WESLEY STEVENS
A. WILCOX FOSTER   A. W. WILCOX
WALTER R. HORLACHER

Sophomores

J. FARR BROWN   E. D. McCOLLUM
CARROL L. LUND   HERBERT V. MERING
JOHN F. NOVAK   N. DALE LUND
NATHANIEL P. WOODS

Freshmen

LeROY M. LEITER   PAUL KOVAR
RALPH M. MURRAY   NORMAN W. HEIM

Pledges

R. RUSSELL FULLER   MARTIN E. KNOLD
CARL A. KRETH   DURLAND J. HILTS

Frater in Facultate

P. J. NEWMAN

Frater in Urbe

CAMERON S. GOLDSMITH

Alpha Theta Chi

Top row—BROWN, LUND, WOODS, FOSTER, MURRAY, LEITER, KOVER
Middle row—HEIM, McCULLOM, NEWMAN, ANGLE, LUND
Bottom row—FULLER, RODEWALD, WILCOX, HORLACHER

Pi Kappa Alpha

Founded at the University of Virginia, 1868.

Alpha Omega Chapter

Installed June 14, 1913

Publications—"Shield and Diamond" and "Dagger and Key"

Flower—Lily of the Valley.   *Colors*—Garnet and Old Gold.

MEMBERS

Seniors

COLEMAN WHITE MCCAMPBELL

Juniors

GEORGE LOWELL KELLEY   RALPH DAMEN NIXON
LESTER FRANK GFELLER   HAROLD STEPHEN WOODARD
                 LOREN VAN ZILE

Sophomores

FRANK HOATH   CLAIRE ANSEL DOWNING
                     MERTON LOUIS OTTO

Freshmen

HERBERT SAWYER FRENCH   HORACE RANDELS
CARL UHLRICH   CECIL MOORE

Fratres in Facultate

LYNDELL PORTER WHITEHEAD   LYMAN R. VAWTER
RAY I. THROCKMORTON   WALDO E. GRIMES
                 EUSTIS V. FLOYD

Pi Kappa Alpha

Top row—HOATH, NIXON
Second row—DOWNING, MOORE, KELLEY, FRENCH
Third row—GFELLER, VAWTER, UHLRICH, RANDELS, VAN ZILE
Bottom row—OTTO, McCAMPBELL, WOODWARD, WHITEHEAD

Men's Pan-Hellenic Council

Top row—ROCHFORD, GILBERT
Second row—MYERS, KNISELEY, RYAN
Third row—WOODWARD, MACGREGOR, O'BRIEN, HORCHFIELD
Bottom row—OTTO, RITTER, MILLER

The Men's Pan-Hellenic Council is an organization which governs the social fraternities at the college in all matters of common interest and which co-operates with the college authorities on matters of fraternity concern.

MEMBERS

Acacia
H. D. RYAN
H. W. HORSFIELD

Beta Theta Pi
L. R. RITTER
C. H. MYERS

Pi Kappa Alpha
H. S. WOODWARD
M. E. OTTO

Sigma Alpha Epsilon
H. R. GUILBERT
L. H. ROCHFORD

Sigma Nu
H. A. O'BRIEN
C. P. MILLER

Sigma Phi Epsilon
C. C. KNISELEY
R. D. MACGREGOR

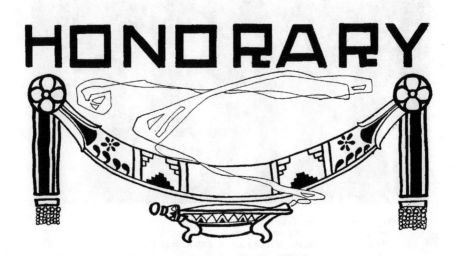

Omicron Nu

Top row—SLOOP, OLMSTEAD, HERRICK, BERRY
Middle row—SAMUELS, TAYLOR, HEISER, VANDERWILT, BLAIR
Bottom row—ORR, LATZKE, JOHNSON, LATZKE, RUSSELL, HALL

Honorary Home Economics Fraternity
Founded at Michigan Agricultural College, April 23, 1912.

Kansas Theta Chapter
Installed May 31, 1915.

Colors—Pink and Lavender.   *Flower*—Sweet Pea.

MEMBERS

In Facultate

MRS. BIRDSALL   MISS HAGGART   MISS MCCOY
MISS COX   MRS. VAN ZILE   MISS LLOYD-JONES
                       MISS WITHAM

Active Members

MILDRED BERRY   SARELLA HERRICK   ALPHA LATZKE
RUTH BLAIR   EDITH HALL   ESTHER LATZKE
RUTH ORR   FRANCES RUSSELL   VERA SAMUEL
LUCILLE HEISER   GUSSIE JOHNSON   VERA OLMSTEAD
LOLA SLOOP   MYRTLE VANDERWILT   RUTH TAYLOR

Pledges

DR. HELEN B. THOMPSON EDNA WILKIN   LAVERNE WEBB
GLADYS GANSHIRD   MISS COWLES   HELEN DAWLEY
JESSIE HIBLER   GLADYS LOVE

Alpha Zeta

Top row—FRED GRIFFEE, CHAS. SWINGLE, W. W. BELL, L. V. RITTER
Second row—A. W. FOSTER, E. S. LYONS, E. F. WHEDON, O. STEANSON, E. J. PRICE
Bottom row—E. E. GOTTMAN, B. F. AGNEW, G. Y. BLAIR, W. C. JANSSEN, J. B. ANGLE

Alpha Zeta was founded at Ohio University, 1897, and has grown now until it has twenty-six chapters.

MEMBERS IN FACULTATE

W. M. JARDINE
C. W. McCAMPBELL
L. D. BUSHNELL
J. T. WILLARD
L. A. FITZ
ALBERT DICKENS
M. F. AHEAN
R. K. NABOURS
G. A. DEAN
E. C. MILLER
J. C. CUNNINGHAM
W. A. LIPPENCOTT
E. F. FERRIN
H. B. WINCHESTER

J. H. PARKER
L. E. CALL
RALPH KENNY
W. L. SATSHAW
R. I. THROCKMORTON
J. B. FITCH
F. W. BELL
A. G. HOGAN
H. J. BOWER
G. E. THOMPSON
M. C. SEWELL
H. L. KENT
W. E. GRIMES
P. F. McNALL

L. G. FAIRCHILD

Theta Sigma Phi

Top row—POLSON, CATE, LONG, YOST, CARSON
Bottom row—CORBY, HENDERSON, SHINGLEDECKER, KEELER, MOORE

Theta Sigma Phi which was organized in 1909 is an honorary, professional fraternity composed of women of the School of Journalism.

Colors—Violet and Green.   *Flower*—Violet.
                        Publication—"The Matrix."

MEMBERS

IZIL POLSON
DORA CATE
NADIA DUNN CORBY
RUTH HENDERSON
JEANETTE LONG

SARA CHASE YOST
VELMA CARSON
LAURA SHINGLEDECKER
LAURA DUELLE MOORE
JULIA KEELER

Sigma Delta Chi

Top row—DAVIS, MILLER, BREWER, CRAWFORD
Bottom row—KEITH, BOONE, ENNS, MOORE, HAWKINS

Sigma Delta Chi is an honorary fraternity composed of men who have done distinguished work in the field of journalism.

MEMBERS

H. W. DAVIS		FLOYD HAWKINS
N. A. CRAWFORD		H. T. ENNS
E. T. KEITH		FRANKLIN BOONE
H. A. MOORE		CARL MILLER
	BRUCE B. BREWER	

ALUMNI

D. P. RICORD	E. D. KEILMAN	R. H. HEPPE
T. W. MORSE	G. C. WHEELER	L. C. MOSIER
T. A. LEADLEY	W. A. SUMNER	J. M. BORING
V. V. DETWILDER	T. F. BLACKBURN	B. Q. SHIELDS
B. K. BAGDIGIAN	V. E. BUNDY	ARTHUR BOYER
E. H. SMITH	W. T. BRINK	C. W. HESTWOOD

Zeta Kappa Psi

Top row—SLOOP, DERBY, HARMON, CATE
Bottom row—SAPPENFIELD, CIRCLE, STINSON, SAPPENFIELD, JOHNSON

Honorary Forensic Sorority

MEMBERS

LOLA SLOOP

GRACE DERBY

DORA CATE

JEWELL SAPPENFIELD

ELIZABETH CIRCLE

ELLA STINSON

BLANCH SAPPENFIELD

GUSSIE JOHNSON

Pi Kappa Delta

Top row—THOMPSON, MEDLIN, MACARTHUR, FAIRMAN, HAMILTON
Bottom row—GRIMES, SWANSON, MOORE, BARGER, HAWKINS

Honorary Forensic Fraternity

Founded at Ottawa University, January, 1915

Kansas Gamma Chapter

Colors—Cerise and Cream   *Publication*—"Forensic"

HONORARY MEMBERS

DR. H. J. WATERS   W. E. GRIMES
J. W. SEARSON   L. C. WILLIAMS

ACTIVE MEMBERS

C. J. MEDLIN   TURNER BARGER
DR. J. R. MACARTHUR   H. A. MOORE
A. F. SWANSON   SEIBERT FAIRMAN
J. D. THOMPSON   G. W. HAMILTON
FLOYD HAWKINS   OSCAR STEANSON

Sigma Tau

Top row—VAN TRINE, HAMILTON, LUCAS, SCHULTZ, FETZER, FOLCK, BROWNING, S. A. SMITH
Middle row—BIGGER, R. A. SEATON, J. D. WALTERS, A. A. POTTER, C. E. REID, W. W. CARLSON
Bottom row—McCRACKEN, C. E. PEARCE, PAINTER, WILLIAMSON, HUNT

Honorary Engineering Fraternity

Founded at University of Nebraska, February 22, 1904

Epsilon Chapter Installed May 12, 1919

Colors—Blue and White   *Publication*—"Pyramid"

MEMBERS

Honorary in Facultate

A. A. POTTER	S. A. SMITH
L. E. CONRAD	K. J. T. EKBLAW
J. D. WALTERS	E. E. BAKER
R. A. SEATON	F. F. FRAZIER
C. E. REID	C. E. PEARCE
W. W. CARLSON	H. H. FENTON

J. P. CALDERWOOD

ACTIVE MEMBERS

Seniors

R. A. VANTRINE	S. P. HUNT
J. S. PAINTER	H. G. SCHULTZ
G. W. McCRACKERN	E. T. WILLIAMSON
G. W. HAMILTON	T. W. BIGGER

Juniors

M. J. LUCAS	C. L. BROWNING
P. L. FETZER	R. W. FOLCK

The Honor Society of Agriculture

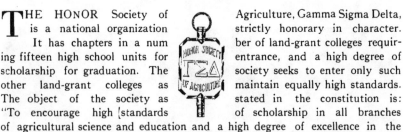

THE HONOR Society of Agriculture, Gamma Sigma Delta, is a national organization strictly honorary in character. It has chapters in a number of land-grant colleges requiring fifteen high school units for entrance, and a high degree of scholarship for graduation. The society seeks to enter only such other land-grant colleges as maintain equally high standards. The object of the society as stated in the constitution is: "To encourage high [standards of scholarship in all branches of agricultural science and education and a high degree of excellence in the practice of agricultural pursuits."

Members of the faculty and alumni engaged in the work of agriculture or in science related to agriculture and who have rendered signal service in the cause of agricultural development are eligible to membership. Only students who are majoring in agriculture or closely related science and whose scholarship records are such as to place them in the upper one-fourth of their class are eligible to membership. Candidates must also be within one semester of graduation and possess, in the estimation of the local society, marked capacity for leadership and efficient service as citizens. Elections are held in April each year.

In the annual elections of April, 1918, and April, 1919, students were elected to membership as follows:

CANDIDATES FOR THE DEGREE OF BACHELOR OF SCIENCE

1918

BENJAMIN FRANCIS BARNES	FRED HARRISON CARP	WALTER WAYNE HOUGHTON
HOBART McNEIL BIRKS	CECIL ORR CHUBB	CHARLES OTIS JOHNSTON
FRANK OTTO BLECHA	MERLE WARREN CONVERSE	RUSSELL MORRISON
ORVILLE THOMAS BONNETT	DAVID EARL CURRY	GLENN CHASE WARE
HELEN FAIRBANKS CARLYLE	NEIL EDWIN DALE	JAMES WALTER ZAHNLEY
	CARL LAWRENCE HEDSTROM	

1919

JAMES BELL ANGLE	GEORGE YOEMAN BLAIR	FRANK SWARTZ CAMPBELL
SHIRLEY BLANCH FRENCH	FRED GRIFFEE	FLOYD MEREDITH PICKRELL
EVERETT JACOB PRICE	FRANK C. WILSON	

GRADUATE STUDENTS

1918

LEVI JACKSON HORLACHER
JAY LAURENCE LUSH
WILLIAM PRESTON TUTTLE

1919

STELLA MAUDE HARRISS

MacDowell Club

Top row—Hoots, Abernethy, Kimmel, Klotz, Colburn, Klotz
Bottom row—Curry, Bauersfield, Hanna, Burris, Rice, Hughes

Organized September, 1918

Colors—Pink and Green   Flower—Sweet Pea

OFFICERS

Nina Bess Curry . . . . President
F. Pearl Hoots . . . . Vice-President
Alena Bauersfield . . . . Secretary
Marie Burris . . . . Treasurer

MEMBERS

Katherine Kimmel
Louise Hughes
Patricia Abernethy
Pearl Hoots
Bernice Klotz
Marie Burris
Helen Colburn

Doris M. Bugbey
Elsie Smith
Nina Bess Curry
Alice Rice
Ollie Klotz
Alena Bauersfield
Lois Hanna

College Activities

1919 Orators

Top row—MEDLIN, BLAIR, NELSON
Bottom row—SWANSON, JOHNSON, TURNER, BENTLEY, BREWER

The intersociety oratorical is one of the big events of the college year. Try-outs are held in each society and the winners meet to decide the best orator on the hill.

ORATORS

Athenian—CALVIN MEDLIN, First Place
Ionian—RUTH BLAIR, Second Place
Hamilton—OLIVER NELSON, Third Place
Webster—BRUCE BREWER
Eurodelphian—GUSSIE JOHNSON
Alpha Beta—W. J. TURNER
Franklin—ARTHUR SWANSON
Browning—MABELL BENTLEY

𝔄𝔤𝔤𝔦𝔢 𝔓𝔬𝔭 𝔑𝔦𝔤𝔥𝔱

A SCENE FROM THE WINNING STUNT "WEDDING IN THE WILDS"

Once each year every student at the Kansas State Agricultural College tries to be clever and originate a winning stunt for Aggie Popularity Night. Each organization on the hill plans a stunt and presents it to a committee which chooses seven to be staged Aggie Pop Night. The organization presenting the most clever and original stunt receives a silver loving cup to hold until another Pop Night. This cup was given to the cause by the Y. W. C. A. Advisory Board. This year the cup went to the Eurodelphian Literary Society.

The President's Inauguration

This year the history of K. S. A. C. will be marked by the inauguration of William M. Jardine, the seventh president of K. S. A. C.

During his association with the college, President Jardine has won a lasting place in the hearts of the students by the "Pep" and never failing interest he shows in college activities. Under his leadership the future of K. S. A. C. is assured.

Dr. Raymond A. Pearson, president of the Iowa State College, was the principal speaker of the inaugural exercises.

The inaugural banquet was prepared and served in the domestic science dining room by the Institutional Management girls.

A reception was held in the Gymnasium at night. Faculty members and representatives from over the state were guests.

Men's Pentangular Debate

Resolved: That the League of Nations as advocated by President Wilson is a practicable way of securing permanent peace.

SQUAD

SEIBERT FAIRMAN	S. J. GILBERT
L. WHEARTY	C. GRAVES
L. C. BINFORD	H. E. MATHER
R. S. CIRCLE	E. R. SWEET
A. J. ENGLUND	H. E. MOORE

K. S. A. C.—Washburn Debate

Resolved: That the League of Nations to enforce peace is a practicable method of securing permanent peace.

SQUAD

MYRTLE GUNSELMAN	LOLA SLOOP KKK
FLORENCE MATHER	BLANCH SAPPENFIELD KK
DOROTHY MOSELY	CHRISTINE COOL

𝕶. 𝕾. 𝕬. 𝕮.—Ames Debate

Resolved: That the single tax on land should be substituted for all other forms of state and local taxation. Constitutionality waived.

A. Graham   J. W. Barger
C. C. McPherson   W. B. Horlacher
C. J. Medlin, K. K.   E. H. Willis
N. J. Lucas   E. J. Price
Earl Frost   O. Nelson
Oscar Steanson   Turner Barger
              Floyd Hawkins

𝕶. 𝕾. 𝕬. 𝕮.—Hays Normal

SQUAD

JEWEL SAPPENFIELD K

IRENE GRAHAM

LUCRETIA SCHULER

ELIZABETH CIRCLE K

ELLA STINSON K

ELIZABETH COTTON

MARY HILL

CHRISTEL ATCHISON

MABEL BENTLY

CLARA HOWARD

GRACE TURNER

CLEMENTINE PADDLEFORD

OLIVE LOGERSTROM K

Debate Council

Top row—SLOOP, CARRIS, CIRCLE, FAIRMAN, MEDLIN, JOHNSON, HAMILTON, CATE
Bottom row—MOSELEY, CIRCLE, WHEARTY, HILL, MOORE, COOL, FROST, GUNSELMAN, LUCAS

The Debating Council is composed of two representatives from each literary society. These representatives act for their society in deciding all matters concerning debate.

REPRESENTATIVES

Brownings
> HETTIE CARRIS
> MYRTLE GUNSELMAN

Athenian
> CALVIN MEDLIN
> SEIBERT FAIRMAN

Eurodelphian
> CHRISTINE COOL
> GUSSIE JOHNSON

Websters
> EARL FROST
> L. WHEARTY

Ionian
> DORA CATE
> ELIZABETH CIRCLE

Hamiltons
> GORDON HAMILTON
> RAY CIRCLE

Alpha Beta
> WESLEY LUCAS
> DOROTHY MOSELY

Franklins
> HARRY MOORE
> MARY HILL

Royal Purple Staff

Top row—OLMSTEAD, HAMILTON, GRAMSE, FAIRMAN, HERRICK, CARSON
Middle row—SLOOP, COTTON, MYERS, YOST, WEBB, BLAIR
Bottom row—BORTHWICK, JOHNSON, TAYLOR, HALLECK, THOMAS, BREWER

STAFF

VERA OLMSTEAD	*Business Manager*
VELMA CARSON	*Editor*
RUTH BLAIR	*Assistant Business Manager*
GREETA GRAMSE	*Treasurer*
GORDON HAMILTON	*Assistant Business Manager*
SARELLA HERRICK	*Military Editor*
BRUCE B. BREWER	*Assistant Military Editor*
SARA CHASE YOST	*Art Editor*
ELIZABETH COTTON	*Class Editor*
MARTHA WEBB	*Advertising Manager*
SIBERT FAIRMAN	*Assistant Advertising Manager*
GUSSIE JOHNSON	*College Year Editor*
RUTH THOMAS	*Women's Athletics*
LUCILE HALLECK	*View Editor*
RUTH BORTHWICK	*Aggie Girl Editor*
LOLA SLOOP	*Snapshot Editor*
CLIFF MYERS	*Athletic Editor*
RUTH TAYLOR	*Cartoons*

The Ides of March

We got to saying "Hell, Yes!" at pep meetings and then we thought up Rough Neck day. The first sign of spring at K. S. A. C. is a poster on the bulletin board warning the public to beware of the Ides of March. Because the Ides of March are considered more dangerous than the city police, on the day of the fifteenth, the populace comes out dressed fit to be killed.

Coxey's army would have blushed like a spring dawn to see K. S. A. C. so out at the elbows. Everyone comes to school dressed like they used to at home on the farm—each looks as brainless as he naturally is.

However, it is the one day in all the year that we shabby ones need not be envious. It is a day when we better dressed ones are brought to realize the real insignificance of silk and fine linen. It adjusts our sense of values. It brings us all together. It justifies its existence.

May Fete

When spring comes to the campus at K. S. A. C., it brings with it the beautiful custom of crowning the Queen of May. A senior girl is chosen by the student body to reign for a day. From her throne she reviews the graceful dances, mad frolics and joyous games of her subjects. In gay procession they pass beneath the campus trees and play on the campus green. Then, just before the sun reddens the west, boys and girls wind the May pole and May day becomes another happy college memory.

Inter=Fraternity Basket Ball

U NUSUAL interest was manifested this year by the national fraternities in the contest for the basket ball championship cup which is presented annually to the winner by the Pan-Hellenic Council. This interest was due largely to the uncertainty of the final result, the strength of each team being an unknown quantity, the outcome being further complicated by the addition of a new member to the Council, the Sigma Phi Epsilon fraternity.

In 1917 the Aztex fraternity, which was at that time a member of the Council, won the championship Last year the Sigma Nu fraternity came into possession of the cup as winner of the contest. To have the trophy as a permanent object of pride and glory it must be won three times by any one of the contestants. No organization has yet succeeded in getting its name on the cup more than once. However, the Sigma Phi Epsilon fraternity made a flying start this year by winning every game and the championship with a total score of 72 as against a total of 29 made by all of its opponents.

The success of the team was due largely to the work of "Susie" Sears who played an invincible game. "Ship" Winter was also a bulwark of strength for the Sig Eps before he became ineligible because of playing on the varsity squad. The other members of the Championship quintet were Fairman, Janssen, Haughton, Knisely, Raymond and MacGregor.

Kansas State Collegian

BARKER   SCHEMONSKI   PADDLEFORD   MYERS   WADLEY   ENNS   MILLER

CARL P. MILLER . . . . . *Business Manager*
ELIZABETH WADLEY . . . . *Editor, First Semester*
IVYL BARKER . . . . . *Editor, Second Semester*
H. T. ENNS, JR. . . . . . *Associate Editor*
C. H. MYERS . . . . . . *Sport Editor*
BENNIE SCHEMONSKI . . . . *Circulation Manager*
CLEMENTINE PADDLEFORD . . . . *Society Editor*

The Kansas State Collegian is the official student publication of the college. It is published each Tuesday and Friday of the school year and contains all the news of, or especially interesting to the students and faculty of K. S. A. C. There are usually feature stories and special articles about the college in general. Besides the college public, it goes to more than four hundred and twenty-five high schools of the state.

NSAS STATE COLLEGIAN

KANSAS STATE AGRICULTURAL COLLEGE
E CENTS

AGGIES F
AST AND B
NFIDENT O

James Wit
and Saturd
the Valley
ship.

Will the Aggies be able to li
Hoosiers back in two hard
games, and thus capture the championship of the valley Hell Yes! at
least that is the way every Aggie student feels, and in the way that the
most of the sport writers of the valley have figured.

K. U. Victory Big Upset.

The K. U. victory over Neb
Wednesday was pretty much
pset in dope, although Coach
art of Nebraska used his s
string men all during the first
in order to save his stars for the
ole games. Even at that, the sc
31 to 17 by which the Kansa
feated Nebraska surely point
some weakness in the Nebraska

As neither Coach Clevenger
Coach Scholz have seen the H
in action, no one can be gott
their strength, except through
sport sheets of the various t
Such dope, however, points t
fact that Nebraska's strong po
her teamwork. Also that the team
while not as large as the usual Husk-
er teams, is unusually fast.

Nebraska Plays Rough Game.
The Nebraskans also play a close

MEE

BALL T
EP FOR

Abearn
dy For th
ionship—T

Teaches Interesting
Facts About Insects

Are you acquainted with the fact that
certain gnats vibrate their wings
and that a com-
ing bird is some-
eyes, or that a
musoles?
n other actions
nd in the gen-
ure which is
A. Dean. Few
f many curious
to be found out
e and habits of
insects which

many students
of insects is us-
hly loged with
ater-bootles and
by coming to
aker and lifting
thus forcing
a cavity beneath them into which
the air rushed.? These insects can
then swim through the water carrying this air with them in a position
where it can be respired. When the

WING
BAISE

ing! When? Friday the third hour!
Where? The Auditorium! What for?
Just to decide how badly the college
wants the boys to beat Nebraska,
what kind of a celebration there is
to be after the game Saturday night,
whether the college is to have any
baseball this spring and a few other
questions.

Profs. to Give Short Talks.

This is going to be one of the big-
gest pep log ether meetings in the history of the school, according to the
men behind the idea, and it is for a
big goal, the Missouri Valley championship, and a season of baseball.
The band will be there and in action
and three of the best liked men of
the faculty will give short talks.

Coach Clevenger, the man who has
put the Aggie team on the map, and
to whose coaching the present success of the team is due, will give the
first address. Mike Ahearn and Professor King will be right there to
start the old time pep going and they
will start it too, from what the pro-
moters of the pep meeting say.

Baseball This Spring?

Drake, Mabel Dial
Sophomores:
**Forwards—Florence Banker, Edna
Engle. Guards—Clementine Paddi-
ford, Helen Sloan, Gladys Turner.**

Helping Rebuild Country Wrecked
By War—Near Swiss Border.

James A. Hall, '17, is with the
Friends' Reconstruction unit in
France. He writes to Dr J. E. Kam-
meyer:

W. O. McCarty, sophomore in agriculture, who has been out of college the past week on account of
eye trouble, returned to resume his
college, this morning.

R. Sweet, '17, of the 45th
amp Gordon, Georgia,
y in Manhattan visiting
Eugene Sweet. Captain
his way to California.

Unventilated Room
Causes Students
To Get Low Grades

Determinedly the sleepers arouse
and make stern resolves to stay
awake. The hour seems interminably
long; eyelids weigh a ton. One
student fighting a terrific battle for
consciousness and a grade—sleepily
rhymes:

The bravest battles that ever were
fought
Were not on the fields "over there"

The Morning After · Phew! · Rail Walking · Gossips · I Need Help · Gertrude · Aid · What · Prix

Aggie Girls

They are typical all-round, loyal
Aggie Girls—all six of them—
for the college voted them so.

Hazel Taylor

Lola Sloop

Velma Larson

Mary Mason

Ruby Zrucker

HIXON-CONNELLY STUDIO.

Ada Robertson

HIXON-CONNELLY STUDIO.

One's character and likeness
reflected in the camera
with thought and art is the
effort of

The Hixon-Connelly
Studios
"Photographers of Distinction"

Studio
Lobby Baltimore Hotel
Kansas City
Photographers for 1919
Aggie Girls

ΠΚΑ

Kitty   Mascots   Harold

Shinning Up   Trio   Dolled Up

GAMES

Football

1919 Football

A T THE beginning of the football season of 1918 the Aggie lineup of
prospects seemed rather depleted. Although there were forty men out for
the first practice, these men for the most part lacked experience. Some
had played on high school teams for four years and some had come from
other colleges, but still there was a doubt as to whether the Missouri Valley
conference would allow first year men to play on the Varsity teams. Old men
were a minus quantity. Gatz, Husted, Bogue, Hinds were the only letter
men that returned to resume their studies.

Around these four men as a nucleus Coach Clevenger and Assistant-Coach
"Germany" Shulz built a team that, had it been allowed to finish the season
would have run Kansas University a close race for the championship of the
Valley. After the first three games had been played Hinds who was showing
better form than he had the year before and Murphy, one of the strongest
centers the Aggies have had in many years were called to training camps and
the coaches had to find new material to fill the places made vacant by these
two veterans.

Throughout the entire season new difficulties were presenting themselves
that made it no easy task for the coaches to keep a team going regular. First
the organization of the S. A. T. C. interfered with the practice hours, then
came the news that some of the men who had expected to play would drop out
on account of injuries received in previous years or on account of studies. On
top of all this the influenza epidemic broke out and on that account several
of the scheduled games had to be cancelled. Practice games went by as if
nothing had interfered.

The Kansas University-Kansas Aggie game was the big contest of the season
and was played on the Kansas gridiron on Thanksgiving day. The field was
covered with water and the Aggie team was light. The old jinx at this time
twelve years old was still with the Aggie and the game was lost to Kansas,
13 to 7. The football season ended with the fans hoping that the jinx might
be broken in 1919, the thirteenth year of its existence.

Schedule of Games

September 28—Aggies	22	Baker	0
October 5—Aggies	27	Ft. Riley	7
November 9—Aggies	28	Washburn	9
November 23—Aggies	11	Ames	0
November 28—Aggies	7	Kansas	13
Totals	95		29

FOOTBALL—Continued

"Johnnie" Clarke, K. S. A. C.'s all around athlete is the same star in football that he is in basketball and baseball. Johnnie has the Aggie spirit and he puts it across. Unfortunately this is his last year.

"Smoky Hill" Bogue, captain-elect of the 1919 team has all the spirit in the universe and with Joe at the head of the Aggie aggregation Coach Clevenger expects to have one of the most perfect machines that have ever existed in the Missouri Valley conference, next year. Joe has two more years of Aggie football before him. In those two years he will show the Valley a real end.

Cliff Gallagher, the speedy Oklahoman who first played on the Aggie gridiron as an opponent with the Oklahoma Aggies in 1916 is one of the fastest, brainiest and smallest halfbacks that the Wildcats have possessed for several years. Cliff was easily persuaded to change Aggie schools and has already established himself as one of the necessities of the future success of the Purple football.

To find a better, bigger guard than "Ike" Gatz would require a thorough search of the largest schools in the country. Ike after playing a good game on the Freshmen Varsity in 1916 at center was transferred the next year to guard on the Varsity. This year he not only held down the left guard position but was chosen unanimously as the captain of the Aggie S. A. T. C. team.

Young playing beside Gatz made a wonderful combination of weight endurance and fight on the left side of the line, a combination that only very few opponents could break through. Young came to the Aggies from the Kansas City Veterinary College. He is a Senior but is thinking seriously of refusing the diploma in order to play with the best team in the Valley next year.

THE BIG
FIVE

ALL-VALLEY
SELECTIONS

FOOTBALL—Continued

'Pete" Hixson, a junior vet, showed a wonderful development this year in the half-back position. Pete, last year was one of the best "subs" that Coach Clevenger carried on his trips; this year he was one of the best half-backs in the Valley, next year the Wildcats will place great confidence in this small but mighty Wild-kitten.

"Ship" Winters, playing his first year of college football, made one of the fastest, hardest hitting ends in the Missouri Valley this year. His play was both sure and spectacular. Ship could be depended upon to get his man on every play around his end. Three years more of college football lies before this man and he is expected to make one of the best athletes the Kansas Aggies ever turned out.

Husted, "Hustey" for short, playing at the full-back position was to be counted on for five yards at any time that the team needed it and was a consistent ground gainer for the Aggies. Several times when the Aggies needed only a few feet to make a touchdown, Husted was called upon to make the gain and was successful.

"Mac" Magrath played as first alternate to right tackle and right guard. His height accompanied with a grim determination to get the other fellow has won for Mac a name that the Aggies will retain in their memory until football has become one of the middle-age sports.

"Ding" Burton, quarter on the Freshman Varsity of 1917, and pilot of the regulars during the S. A. T. C. season of 1918, proved to be one of the mainstays of the Aggie aggregation. Even at times when Ding was "out of his head" on account of injuries, he continued to run the team with the determination that made him one of the selections for the All-Valley quarter position.

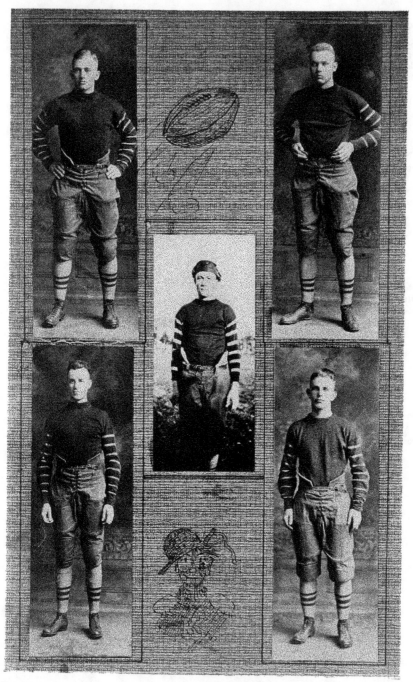

FOOTBALL—Continued

Lloyd Miller at half-back played a game that did justice to the efforts that he put in in practice. Miller is one of the hardest working men that has ever donned an Aggie football uniform and played with a Purple team. After playing a year on the Freshman squad Miller "subbed" a year and then played this year at either half-back position relieving Gallagher and Hixon.

"Chief" alias "Young Stiff" Randals has started to place his name before the Missouri Valley conference along with that of his brother "Stiff" as one of the hardest hitting tacklers and one of the slickest field runners that ever wore the moleskins. His carriage, his hair and his smile are the things that bring back the memory of his older brother.

Dewey Houston was the one man on the team that could be depended upon for three points in almost any football game of the season. His toe was one of the strong points of the Aggie Wildcats. As a guard he was a strong, consistent line plunger.

BAKER-AGGIE GAME '18

THE SQUAD

AGGIE BAND

STOPPED

BURTON AROUND LEFT END

THE LINE HELD

A FLYING TACKLE

NEBRASKANS

Basketball

Basket Ball

A NOTHER championship basket ball team has been added to the list held by the Kansas Aggies. At the opening of the season it was predicted that the Purple five would clean up on the valley and they did. The season started with a rush. It was an easy matter for the Aggies to clean up on the teams from Fort Riley and St. Marys and Camp Funston. The Emporia Normals, high in the State Championship race, were also added to the string of unsuccessful opponents.

The season started with one of the best teams of the valley and the Aggies were again successful, this time downing Kansas University twice in as many games. Then followed the remainder of teams in the valley. No team showed the Aggies a hard battle until Nebraska invaded the Nichols court and put up a likely scrap. Two games were taken from this team, one of the contenders for the "rag."

The victorious season continued until the champions met Missouri on the court at Columbia. The Aggies seemed to care little for the all-victorious season after the championship had been won. Both games were lost to the Missouri team without a struggle, but the Aggies had annexed another championship.

Next season will be another good season for the Purple team. Plenty of good material is available from this year's Freshman team. A number of the old men of the former Aggie teams will be returned to school by that time and another championship is predicted for the Kansas State College.

George Blair in his second year with the squad has shown the Aggie rooters that it pays to stick to the game thru various odds. Blair graduates this spring and will not be in the team next year.

"Mac" McCullom was another one of the men who helped to make two championship teams possible for the Aggies. After returning from the army Mac donned a suit and made the guards play to gain their position. Mac will be a member of the squad about which Coach Clevenger will build another championship team in 1920.

"Ship" Winter didn't know at the first of the year that he could play basket ball, but after playing half the season with the scrubs he was transferred to the Varsity and played a good game at center. Next year "Ship" will be running someone a stiff race for the right guard position.

Kecker played on the championship team two years ago that won their last two games from Missouri and again helped the Aggies to obtain the rag. Keck entered school late but worked into shape in a very short time and played in every game after the middle of the season.

"Shorty" Foltz won't be back again. This is his last year for the Aggies. He was another veteran of the championship team. As a running mate for Kecker, "Shorty" has shown his ability and has shown his willingness to help make for the Aggies the best team in four states.

BASKET BALL—Continued.

Captain "Johnny" Clarke playing his third year of College Basket Ball at right guard has proven himself to be the best guard in the valley this year. "Johnny" besides being a steady consistent guard is a basket tosser of no small reputation. It is his policy to get at least two or three baskets during the course of the game.

To find a team mate for the captain was the difficulty that confronted the coaches when the season opened. In "Shorty" Cowell was found all that was wanted, a man that could hold anything if necessity demanded and could go down and toss a basket.

Along with other Freshmen in 1917 came a man whom they called Jennings. He was reputed as having been the best high school center in Kansas. After playing one year on the Freshman team he was given his chance with the Varsity and has made good. Jenks is so tall that he shoots baskets over his opponents heads and gets the tip-off with ease.

Another first year man that has proven himself is "Ham" Bunger. "Ham" hails from Colorado, but the Aggies claim him for their own and are proud to do it. A quick, fast, hard playing forward that has not yet found his equal in the Missouri Valley—that's Bunger.

"Heine" Hinds, playing his second year at the forward position, is still going with the speed that has characterized his playing in the three years he has been in school. Heinies floor work has gained for him a reputation as one of the shiftiest of basket ball players.

BASKET BALL

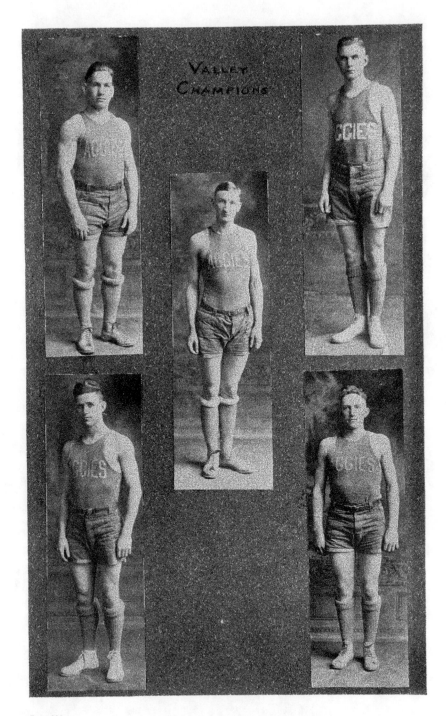

FORT RILEY
M.O.T.C.

SMASHING THE LINE

AGGIE LINE HOLDS

AROUND RIGHT

HOLD 'EM GANG

TOUCHDOWN

AGGIES VISIT K.U.

Track

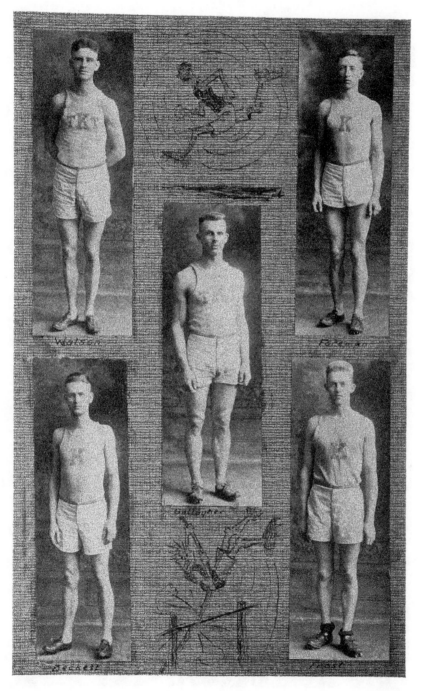

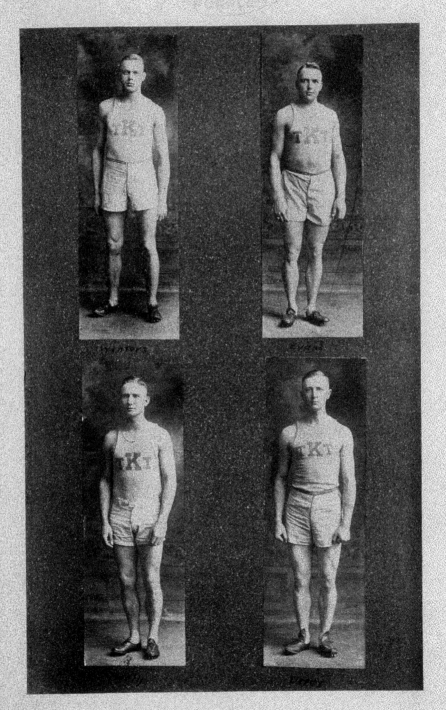

Track

THE TRACK season of 1919 at Kansas State opened with more men out for the team than any other year previous. However the material that appeared seemed to lack experience and confidence in themselves.

Captain Foreman and Frost were the only two men back that had had experience on the Varsity team.

The season opened with Kansas in an indoor meet in the Nichols gymnasium. The Kansans were easily outclassed, the Purple speedsters carrying away the honors in the dashes, the hurdles, the shot put, the mile and the two-mile events and placing in all the other events. The final score of the meet was 28 2-3 for Kansas to 36 1-3 for the Aggies.

The feature meet of the season was the K. S. A. C. meet held in the Convention Hall at Kansas City where the Aggie dash man, Gallagher, broke the world's record in the 50-yard low hurdles and where the Aggies carried away more points than any other organization represented. Watson took a first in the mile, Foreman won the three points in the same race, Beckett took third in the half-mile and Frost tied with Powell of Missouri for second in the pole vault. "Jack" Evans who two years ago was the fastest high school dash man in the state donned Aggie colors when the outdoor practice began and has been showing good form. "Ship" Winters out for the quarter-mile showed good material and will make a good runner for the 1920 team. Tom Neely after the entrance of Evans into the game devoted all of his time to the quarter-mile and has been showing good form. Frost has been making eleven feet consistently this year and expects to do better next year in the pole vault. Depuy is one of the contestants for the quarter-mile who is making good in his race. Captain Foreman still has his equal in the two-mile to meet. He has not yet been defeated in a conference meet.

Prospects point to a great team for the 1920 track team. More material will be available from the Freshman class than ever before and some old men will be back.

Senior Women's Athletics

HOCKEY TEAM

BASKET BALL TEAM

Junior Women's Athletics

BASKET BALL TEAM

HOCKEY TEAM

Intensibe Pocational Courses

THE AGRICULTURAL COLLEGE interests hundreds of men and many young women each year in Special Intensive Courses related to Engineering, the practical intensive work of the Housekeepers' Course and the Farmers' Short Course, and the technical training provided in the Commercial Creamery Short Course.

The special courses related to Engineering train auto mechanics, tractor operators, carpenters, blacksmiths, machinists, foundrymen, telegraphers and electricians. Students may enroll to prepare for any one of the first six vocations named on the first Monday in any month from September to May, inclusive. Each student devotes his entire time to training in his chosen field and usually continues the work until he has acquired the proficiency desired, whether that be for two three, or more months. This method of training practical mechanics was fully developed and its effectiveness proved in the training of thousands of men in the vocational sections of Uncle Sam's army. This year has proved that it is just as applicable and efficient in the training of civilians. In the courses in electrical repair work, radio and telegraphy, students may enroll only on the first Monday of January.

The Housekeepers' Course provides special training in home making. It is given during the first fifteen weeks each semester.

The Farmers' Short Course embraces the most intense and practical work in all phases of farming of economic importance in Kansas. The Commercial Creamery Short Course is a technical course for creamery men. These courses are given during the months of January and February each year, enrollment day being the first Monday in January.

The value to the state of this practical and intensive training in farming, home making, and the various phases of farm engineering given each year to men and women, mostly those actually engaged in the farming industry, can hardly be estimated. Many students, having become acquainted with the work offered, return to the College a second and third time, each time taking new work valuable to them in their vocations. Having completed this second course, they select a third.

The popularity of these courses was demonstrated by the large attendance this year. In spite of unsettled conditions—the war situation and resulting scarcity of labor, and the serious health situation throughout the state during much of the winter—more than three hundred civilian students enrolled in these courses. This enrollment was increased during the month of January by more than two hundred and fifty soldiers from Camp Funston. The picture on the following pages was taken January 27, 1919. It shows two hundred and fifty soldier students and about as many civilians. In the front row of the soldier group may be seen their officers in charge. In the front row of the civilian group are the members of the College faculty especially concerned with the work of these students.

Short Course Students

Pomology Laboratory

Indoor Clinic

Class on a Field Trip

Laboratory in Advanced Crops

Poultry Outdoor Lab Work

Creamery Churn Room

After Student's Judging Contest

Veterinary Dissecting Laboratory

Class in Egg Candling

Class Ready for a Field Trip

Preparing Horses For Show

College Sheep on Campus

College Greenhouses

Antitoxin Cholera Serum Plant

Scene At Poultry Farm

Canary Belt State Butterfat Champion

Wheatfield On The College Farm

Veterinary Hall

A Group of Prize Winners

A Champion Shorthorn Steer

"When the Frost is on the Punkin"

Hostive Handed

Bringing in the Sheaves

Shocked

In the Good Old Summertime

Nurse

No Race, Suicide, Tagel

Purple Cow

I NEVER SAW A PURPLE COW
  I NEVER HOPE TO SEE ONE—
BUT I CAN TELL YOU ANYHOW
  I'D RATHER SEE THAN BE ONE

IF you happen to "be one" in the following pages, accept all congratulations with a grin. Possibly by letting this stuff slip through my fingers I dig my own grave, but said grave don't look half bad. Pasting snapshots alone has made any kind of nemesis look weak. I have not noticed what is going into this section. I am sending the dope to the printer in a gunny sack. It's your misfortune if they shake you out. Don't expect the milk of human kindness from the Purple Cow, and don't trouble to hunt me down. I am

> too proud to fight,
> too poor to bribe,
> too old to care,
> too tired to run
> and too much of a lady
> to say what I think.
>
> —*The Editor*.

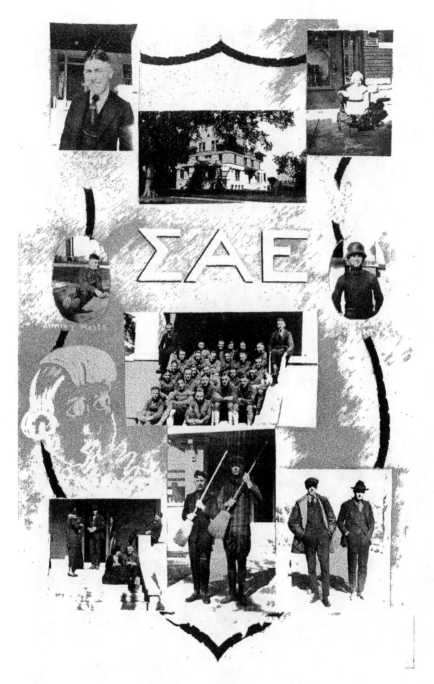

One day it snowed

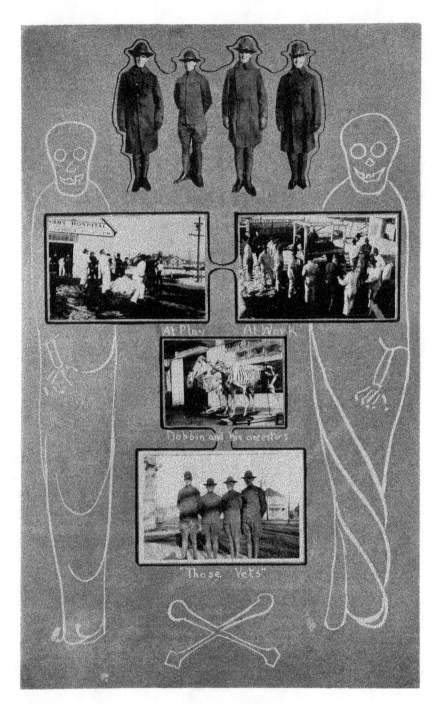

At Play   At Work

Dobbin and his ancestors

"Those Vets"

Gathering Crumbs from the Faculty Table

THE college hill was barren of the things that make it glad.
Those who could had gone to war; the others wished they had.
All traditions were about to gasp their last and die,
But the class of 1919 couldn't let the book go by.
So they fixed up a committee with instructions to go see
A few of the high moguls about whether it should be.
The moguls stroked their furrowed brows and then with judgment rare
They impressed the young committee with the troubles they'd ensnare.
Each had a different "idee" as to what the book should hold
(Their suggestions were so waterproof the campus must be told.)

N. A. Crawford, head professor of the Journalism crowd, pointed out the details, in a speech he gave aloud, to the open-mouthed committee that lined up in his room, of the anguish, and the struggle, and dark and deepening gloom, they were likely to encounter if they undertook a book. "Now a four-page balanced sheet of the perfection and the style of the accurate Industrialist would beat a book a mile. With some interviews on something, bits of verse, some sage, some free, an editorial or so on cigarettes and tea. And the college shop would print it at a nifty little gain"—Then one of the committee noticed it was going to rain.

NOBODY CAN READ EM

THEY waited then until they had an afternoon to spare very an bravely marched into meet Dean Willard in his lair. His attitude was cheerful. He considered that the cash might every bit as well be spent for annuals as trash. A necessary evil this we had to grin and face, just so the editors and staff would conserve extra space. The awful waste in snap shots was a nightmare to the dean. He hitched his glasses up and vowed they never could be seen. Now he'd suggest that snapshots be replaced with thoughtful rhyme. Then one of the committee rose and thanked him for his time.

Well, Prexy took about a week to think the matter o'er and then he called the waiting three inside his office door. He cleared his throat and shook their hands and bade them feel at home and closed his eyelids half way while he said his little poem. He cautiously admitted it a most unusual year. His-

torians with books to write would always hold it dear. And the class of 1919 should some way celebrate its own existence on the hill somehow commemorate the war, or something. Anyhow he had a hazy thought a statue of somebody would be the thing they ought to replace the Royal Purple with —of course he could not tell. Then one of the committee thot she heard the chapel bell.

I KNEW TRANSPORTATION WOULD BE SO DIFFICULT.

THE dean of women next they met to get her best advice. She quite agreed a memory book of some kind would be nice. She felt the girls could do it, scarcity of men was nil, that all it took was brains and wit and business sense and skill. Though the thought of transportation was the thing that made her fear we'd never get them carted from our printing house to here. She had a vision of a mob demanding books with force, and the business manager bringing them from K. C. on a horse. Now she'd suggest that first we find a way to stop the war. Then one of the committee led the others out the door.

Macarthur (knowing all the rules to make guests feel at ease), embarrassed the committee and soon had them all at seas. A portfolio one could roll and fasten to his vest was the kind of Royal Purple this 'perfesser' liked the best. He hoped sincerely nothing rough would this year break in print. There have been jokes you know good folk that had a yellow tint. A little culture (goodness knows nobody has it here) would help the class of '19 to hold the campus dear. Be careful how you say it, and look well to what you say—Then the heedless young committee went and did it their own way.

Rush Week

THE sweet young thing in autumn rain is gently dragged from off the train by gushing ones who feature furs and spattered spats and kitty purrs, a Greek harangue, a place to board, a taste for things they can't afford. They sway the freshman to the car where several other sisters are who smile and lilt and squeal and coo all over her so young and new. They dash her dizzily away to find a place where she can stay and sling her clothes through rushing week through which she dances sick and weak. She gaily flits from house to house in evening dress or georgette blouse and speculates which way she'll go. She trots from dinner to a show, thence to a dance and up at dawn for some wild breakfast on a lawn. She learns the frats and all their rigs, familiarly raves of "Sigs." Then when the last Greek hop is hopped, the poor thing's either pledged or dropped.

Rushees are expected to dance with each other.

The tender youth with knitted brows who just last night was milking cows on father's farm so calm and still was also grabbed against his will, by Greeks, who, taking in his size, see future football in his eyes. They knock his reason off the track by slapping him upon the back so hard his cerebellum shakes and big importance *Nothing* takes. They give a smoker for the boy, and other freshmen young and coy. If that don't start him coming 'long they gently sing the old frat song, administer a social dance where wily co-eds have a chance to help him lose his own good head—and use his pocketbook instead. The little button soon looks good, as wise old brothers knew it would. And when he wakens from the spell, he finds it in his coat lapel.

If the Old Frat House Could Talk

THE artist just fixed me this way so that the public would think I harbor a real fraternity. Shucks, they are nothing but a lot of nice boys—brooded over by Papa Macarthur. He sees that they gargle their throats in winter and makes them put back the money they take as treasurers of organizations. As soon as they get well started they expect to keep a cow and chickens. Yes, the Sig Eps have their faults—had 'em even back in the days when they were tri-nothings. They often interpret Sigma Phi Epsilon as Signify Everything. Well, it takes all kinds of men to make Pan Hell and it didn't take the Sig Eps long.

I'M a pretty decent looking place in real life and I'm going to defend my architecture by explaining that Tom Neely took this picture the morning after he—aw, I guess I won't tell on Tom. What's the soul of a house in comparison to the reputation of a man? No, it wasn't the time he and Carl Miller stayed out all night organizing a high school fraternity. It was another time. But what's the use to roast Tom Neely with material like Rex Maupin under my roof? I let a couple of shingles fall the other day when I heard that Hamilton and Epperson had "cooled" their 3rd chicken in 1919. Only a frat house understands that remark. By the way, the Sigma Nus would give their charter if they could recover the remarks they left at the Chi Omega house the time they went after their furniture. They s'posed there was nobody home. They live under an Italian motto, "Dice et les Dames." There's nothing to do now but let the Sigma Nus stay and thank Heaven there can be only one chapter in one college and not everybody will join them.

P. S.—Hap O'Brien is a Sigma Nu. Always attending some vet convention in Topeka. Now, some fellows—nobody has any idea what course they are taking. Everybody knows, though, that Barringer is taking a dangerous one.

THIS is the more the way I feel than the way I look. I got an idea in my rafters that if the dear brother don't put sand on their shoes the lil' old sign they've hung to my front porch is going to mean not Sigma Alpha Epsilon but Sick And Empty. I consider myself a right spiffy looking house too. I suppose there is nothing for me to do but put on a bold front, stand on the corner and advertise for pledges.

I am not acquainted with my own inmates. They all stay down at the Palace. Dewey McCormick is here at times. They resemble a real fraternity in that they run a table, hold dances and give out pledge buttons. Their pin looks like the ace of diamonds, but there—all this is the Sig Alf's funeral, not mine. I was built to advertise and to shelter any member who should decide to reform and come home.

I AM a fraternity house and I guess, by hek, I look it. I have been through the S. A. T. C. and the spring initiations. I'm simply a nervous wreck from trying to look nice when Delta Tau Delta's were visiting me. The Aztex make me their wigwam. Old Crow Feather (George Blair) is one of the old men who sighs for dimming glory. Heap Big Jerry sits and dreams of days on the western plains. Civilization is plainly getting him. Young Rising Smoke (S. P.) makes good squaw man. They are a race of warriors, these Aztex. They paint 'emselves up with purple K's and scalp anyone who comes across their war path.

ITS superfluous to explain that I am the Beta house and before you get
to wondering what is the matter stop and think who has been living here.

The S. A. T. C. were bad enough, but since Louis Ritter and some of them
came home its been all I could do to keep roof and foundation together.
They say the Betas are strong in K. U. God pity poor old K. U! I know a lot.
Most frat houses do. I know things the discipline committee doesn't. Paw-
huska Smith is one of the best ones and he broke a date with F. R., a sorority
pledge, and she wore crepe on her arm in memory of her dead love. Murphy
Pome de terre ain't so bad.

I missed Heinie Enns one whole day. I found out later when soneome
whispered in my halls that he was doing extension work—was trying to solve
a little problem of how long and thin could you stretch a date without it snapping.
The Kappa cook prepared and served three meals while Heinie sat with B. C.
on the front porch. Finally her pitying sisters lowered a sign from the upper
story announcing that "Quiet Hour" had arrived. I've often wondered what
kind of a sign they lower to get Ike Gatz back from Kansas City, Missouri.
And if there is any sign Shorty Myers could hang before his guardian Angel to
remind her that what Cliff needs is a guardian, not an angel.

THE Sigma Phi Deltas are degenerating beneath my roof. It would be the same under any roof. I refuse to take any of the blame. Well, really, it would be too bad to blame anyone except those who organized it. Its founders got the design for the shield from the Cress Racket Store and chose the colors of a bruise. Their frat song is written to the tune of "Some Sweet Day." There are several Sigma Phi Delts—some besides Gordon—Beaudette is one. Mock is another. There is still another by the name of Francis Totten, candidate for college Sheriff on the platform of free speech. Gordon and the brotherhood joined up because each felt sorry for the other one. There have been worse menaces on the hill—the least I can do is to furnish them a hiding place. The Sigma Phi Delts made the sad mistake of homesteading too far west of the Mississippi, is all.

THERE are worse things than being an Alpha Theta Chi. One of them is being an Alpha Theta Chi house. I speak from sad experience. The Alpha Theta Chis are the only ones of their kind in the United States, but they are petitioning for a charter from the I. W. W.'s. James Angle was an Alpha Theta Chi. Ain't it a shame that Charlie Chaplin can get $10,000 a year for his walk and J. B. has to do his for nothing? The boys justify themselves in being a fraternity. Every now and then a rushee has a fairly good time. And old grads—if they have the nerve and don't care what they do—have a home to come back to. They are very exclusive, which pleases everybody. It would be awful if they went to entertaining their friends. Anything the Alpha Theta Chis could do though would be entertaining. Oh, well, I'd just as soon keep them as regular roomers.

I MAY as well admit that I am the Pi Kappa Alpha house. I guess I look like I've been worrying about them too. I don't know what they put out about themselves, but bless my clapboards, you can take it from me they were founded when no one was looking. The number of chapters is one too many and their colors dark brown. They are noted for wearing stiff upper lips, if you know what I mean by that. It may seem funny, but lots of boys do come to College and pledge Pi Kap. During a lull once they negotiated with the Shamrocks to trade pledges sight unseen, but even the Shamrocks will only go so far. The most prominent members are Woody, Woodward, Harold Woodward, H. S. Woodward and Harold S. Woodward.

Editor's Note—(The Shamrocks promised to pay printing charges on this section if their name and pedigree were kindly omitted. So we didn't say anything about them—but you KNOW—sh).

Dear Bill:

Now I know that there is no use hedgin' with you Bill. I came to this college to join a sorority and I intend to break in somehow. Goodness knows I am not getting very far, but others have done it before me and I wear my ear bobs just as big as any of them.

No, I have not been really rushed. They've all been playing catch with me and about one more strike and I am out. What would it be like to be really *rushed* though? Oh, Sweet Bliss akin only to pledging. I have been to see them all. However, while I was seeing them they were seeing me. It's a kind of a gamble—the outcome depending upon who sees the most. I sure let them all know that I have quite a few dates and that if they took me in they could depend upon a lot of fellows hanging around.

I'm crazy about the Alpha Delts. Say, if I could kid dates out of the men like Murl Gann can I'd be happier. I like the Bachmans too, they aren't so intellectual that it hurts. Nothing crowded there either. You could have a sneak date in the parlor corner and not be apt to be discovered.

I would not mind being a Chi Omega. I wonder if any of them do. Anyhow that have no conscience about asking girls to come in and try it. You used to could tell a Chi Omega by the way she combed her hair, but they've stopped doing that. I asked Gladys Peterson to give me her recipe for getting in but she couldn't, her case was an accident. Jesse Cook dates at their house too. I'm mad about that man's waltz. I love the way he pivots on his heels.

Do you know anything about the Tri Delts, Bill? Most people do, but I'm keen about them anyhow. I like their location. Why do so many of the sororities move so far away from town? I like to live where I can smell the smoke of the drug stores and hear the music from Woodman's hall and get to an ice cream Sundae without getting out of breath.

Still the Kappas have a car or two. They struck luck in Adelaide. They realize it too. I heard at the Kappa house that Van Trine took lessons in love making from the lovely Lou Tellegen. I don't care so much for them tho. Every time you turn around you see a Beta pin. (Marvel sure has a talent for fiances.)

I don't care much for the Pi Phi's either, tho I do admire some of the younger ones. It's just too clever the way they rave about the "SWEET SIG ALPHS." It's pretty awful, Bill, the measures they have to take to have a little mid-week date now and then. One thing I don't like about them is the situation of the porch swings. One of them is right in front of a full length glass door through which the light shines, and I guess the dates that love each other in that porch swing save the people across the street movie money—and give lots of freshmen a wrong idea of college.

Do you know I feel at home at the Delta Zeta House. I love the Wakefield girls' way with the men and I'm mad about Dorothy Gleason's red coat. I wish the D. Z's would invite me home. Oh, well, Bill, it's an ill wind that is too weak to blow and I'll get there yet. I aint had my eyebrows shaved for nothing.

As ever,

MABELLE.

P. S.—There is a bunch of girls that live at 1301 Poynts, Iota Psi, they say, and they are right. I took dinner there. But between you and me, Bill I think that they realize that I am just a little too spiffy for them. With one or two exceptions they wear their own clothes and their only diversions are violet picking and street car rides. They had a fuss about whether they should call themselves "Spunky Spinsters" or "Busy Bees.' So it was a long time before they told anybody they were there and by that time everybody knew it. It came out about the time E. S. threw peas all over the dining room. I don't suppose you are interested though Bill, so I'll ring off. Answer soon.

MAB.

P. P. S.—For heaven's sake don't repeat anything I've said Bill.

M.

The Truth About College Professors

A WORD OF WARNING: We don't advise anybody to be-
come a college professor. It is an awful death. Leave college as
soon as you are graduated. If you hang around a year or two
and soak up a lot of information that you can't throw off, some
desperate board of regents is almost sure to ask you to teach in
their college. And if you accept you are a goner. Afterwards
nobody will ever give you a chance in any line of useful work.

COLLEGE professors, like Gaul and everything else that has ever been written about, are easily divided into three calsses. (It would be just as easy to divide them into four classes, or eleven; but three seems to be the favorite number.) Those three types are old line profs, pink tea profs, and human profs. It is the avowed purpose of this article to discuss them in the order named with impunity, fairness, charity, unction and a lot of other things that we can't take the time to think of now.

The old line professors are almost extinct, and always were. They are usually pale and shelf-worn. They walk with a slight lope, like a coyote, and keep to themselves a great deal. Their hair, when it is worth mentioning, is not worth anything else, bein grassy and anaemic. Their clothes are baggy, because they don't make enough to hire them pressed and their wives are busy doing welfare work or playing auction bridge for 49 cent vases and lace collars. Such profs are nearly always specialists in something or other you have never heard about and never will. They hang out mostly in colleges and college communities where culture is so thick that it won't spread.

The pink tea prof is a different sort of kid, believe him. He dolls himself up like George M. Cohan and cuts up something awful—in his way. He goes in heavy for macaroons and light gray spats and monocles and button-hole bouquets, and adores Water Pater and Freud and Gertrude Stein and Lord Dunsany. He sadly deplores the fact that the great mass of people have common sense instead of erudition. He hardly ever marries—which he shouldn't. Usually he doesn't last long in one place, in which particular he certainly has it on the old line type.

The human professor is not a thing of beauty, but he is a joy forever, bless his heart. He speaks to students, meek and lowly though they are, as if they really had a part to play in this sorry scheme of things. Of course, he is tiresome most of the time, churning over a lot of stuff that doesn't exactly thrill them, but he accepts them as human beings and they forgive him. The only thing really bad about the human prof is that he got a poor start in life.

As a whole, college profs are subject to the same ills and frailties that afflict the ordinary run of mankind. They have boils and indigestion and unruly children, just like anybody else might. They swear at smoky furnaces, fuss with their wives, dodge bill collectors, and stay away from Sunday evening services so that the young folks can go and worship in their own way. On Saturday night after the picture show they bathe in lukewarm water and Ivory soap.

Unless professors see the error of their way and reform before they are fifty, their condition becomes chronic and they gradually go into emeritus and are forced to retire on a princely pension that enables them to have eggs for breakfast once a month for the rest of their natural lives. But if they have been frugal and have denied themselves as nobody can reasonably be expected to do, they can have their homes practically paid for, so we should worry.

Taken all in all, college professors are amicable, single-minded folk, perfectly harmless when they are not taken seriously, which nobody should ever be. The main trouble with so many of them is that they are made—not born.

—*H. W. Davis.*

THE COLLEGE CLUB.

THE College Club is where
Unmarried Profs Hang
Out.
Imagine what
A nestful of them
Would be like.
They swap opinions
On certain students
And
From that time on
The student is done for.
They argue with
Each other
But they don't listen to each other.
They smoke on the front
Porch
And give dances
Sometimes.
They think their
Own methods are
By far
The smartest.

Let others sing of the anguish
Of the S. A. T. C.
As with shaking knees they stand
At inspection,
Awaiting the company commander, and
Their week end sentence.
My song shall be of the maiden
Behind the gun,
The maiden who hopes that his shoes
May be shining,
Who breathlessly wonders whether
His gun is clean,
Who strains limpid eyes to see if his buttons
Are buttoned,
The maiden who prays that her date
May not pass
Into the dim obscurity of the land
That never was.

SOME FIT.

WHEN the S. A. T. C. infested the campus they had quite a lot of fun. One little thing about 'em, their clothes didn't fit. The fat ones were issued tight clothes and the thin ones got clothes that hung on 'em like an unstretched circus tent drapes around the center pole. Their leggins left room for improvement, and several yards of padding. Nothing fit them but the hat cords. It was awful cute of the government to fix them up like that. Everybody thought so. Especially the tailors. Several boys made money —and names for themselves selling fits. Lots of them made names for themselves though, by just walking through Main hall. To hear them from a distance one wouldn't believe that they were just walking through. It sounded as though they were riding through in a horse and buggy that needed greasing.

Their folks sent them money to buy new suits and they had one rare time. Three or four boys, three or four bones, three or four shakes and everybody's money went over the top.

IT BROKE up our college year. It flunked a lot of us. It kept us home for months in sick little towns. It made the Royal Purple and everything else late. It made long distance centrals nervous wrecks. It cost us money, the ordeal of vaccination, and intense anxiety. It took from us many very dear friends—and yet we joke about it. We write silly little poems, and draw ludicrous pictures—shrug our shoulders, and pass on.

Some Line!

Dad: "You've run over your allowance, son."

Son: "Yes, I know it, dad, but I haven't danced, I haven't attended a party, I haven't taken a trip, or done anything but study for the last week; now, dad, please won't you give me enough to get a shoe shine?"

Dad: "Gosh, boy, you're a whang. Here's a twenty, now have a smoke."

Come on Down Perfessor

Why is it that certain members of the faculty deem it necessary to the successful running of this institution that they should sit upon the stage in chapel? Like arch enemies, the faculty and the students—when the latter attend—sit facing each other. This is no royal road to democracy. Why not a shoulder-to-shoulder feeling, with the instructors mixing with the students?

There is still another bad feature of this practice. A certain chapel speaker once said, "Every time I made a statement, I felt those cynical eyes behind me, ready to approve or disapprove, but more ready to disapprove. A man is not afraid of opposition that faces him—it is the dagger in the back that he fears."

And that is probably the sentiment of many men who have made chapel talks.

Good Evidence

Landlady: "Gladys, you stood on the porch quite a while last night with that young man."

Gladys: "Why, my lady, I only stood there for a second.' '

Landlady: "But I'm quite sure I hear the third and fourth."

Alumna
Sometimes
Return

IF THERE is anything alas, that makes a bleak north shiver pass clear up and and down your vertebrae and chills your frame the whole darned way, it's hesitatin' in your track and watchin' poor old grads come back—say one who just three years ago knew everything there was to know, knew everyone by sight and name, whatever happened, they's to blame. Controlled elections, ran the hill, helped turn the wheels in every mill. Who even owned the college pep and never missed a chance to step on freshmen in the way. Well, he slinks back some cloudy day. No one knows him, no one cares. He only gets a few cold stares. He, who a few short years ago, yelled, every step or two, "Hello!" He finds main hall still standing true, the college rushing madly through, folks putting out the same old line, without *him*, things just running fine! He reads in every passing face conviction that he's out of place. He hunts out memories —heaves a sigh as haughty sophomores pass him by.

No there is nothing quite so sad as the return of some old grad.

There was a man in our town,
Oh, he was wondrous wise;
But he jumped into wedlock
For a pair of limpid eyes.

A Slight Difference

Asks the youth who is hearing the call of love,
"What is it that's taking me on?"
Asks the man who has heeded the call of love
"What was it that took me in?"

'NOUGH SAID!

SCANDAL

WE DON'T GIVE A D - - - , WE DON'T

DANCE HALL GIVES SENSATIONS

FRAT LOUNGE LIZARDS AND SOCIAL BUTTER- FLIES ARE CLEVER.

EVERYONE IS INVITED TO THE SENSATIONAL HOP

Strange sights may be seen every Friday and Saturday night at John Harrison's dance hall, when the fraternity lounge lizards and sorority butterflies get together for a little sensational hop.

Many people who are too old to participate but still enjoy the thrills of youth sit on the side lines and observe. Anyone who has a sense of humor is invited. It is a first class show and mighty entertaining. Mrs. Van Zile always attends and usually brings some frivolous member of the faculty with her.

Some of the College people put on more sensational stuff than others. Last Friday night the most amusing thing on the program was the best wabble put on by Harold Combs and Iren Seary. A description of this cannot be given but very likely all of those present remember.

Pi Kappa McCamel bows backward in a peculiar manner that is equal to any Charlie Chapman walk. It gives him a form like question mark.

The Sigma Phi Epsilons are capable of a variety of enterprising stunts, their most successful one however is a glide which they can do very cleverly on the toes of their ladies slippers.

Don Hockomo has some special stuff. He says he learned it at the Blue Goose in Kansas City. You should remember that there are Quackers in our school.

The Delta Zeta's add very little to the entertainment of the specta-

tors, as they usually forget they are at a dance and go to sleep on the bosom of their partner.

Helen Giles comes as often as she can and tries to mix in the men by her temperamental Irish turns. But some of them don't fall for it they say.

Delta Murphy and Kappa Ross are not as frivolous as some of the performers. Their favorite step is a heavy funeral drag, with all the agonies characteristic of the occasion.

Chain and Isabelle gallop merrily around and around the dance hall, always quiet, always looking into space. It is hoped that some time Chain will own an airship so when he wishes to take Isabelle for a soar he may do so in the open where there is plenty of room.

Griff and Anne Wilson take splicing little jig steps, it's all original stuff with them. They believe in conserving good energy for hikes. However that's the Sig Alph's all over.

Sigma Nu Hamilton is crooked. He tries to dance in a circle, but every few minutes he flies off at a tangent and knocks two or three gasping dancers off the floor. But Hamilton may learn yet in the next two years.

If Goddner doesn't stop dancing with her cheek against her partner's she may ruin her dimples. It's hard to give up joys like that but dimples get you farther than La Treble powder.

Everybody does something clever and everybody does something different, it's a fine place to get thrills and ideas.

The faculty are cordially invited to the dances, a hot time is promised. Come on out.
For why should you sit in the scorner's seat,
And hurl the cynic's ban?
Come on out and sit on the seats at Johnies
And be a friend to man.

Sissy Andrews broke into the Chi Omega sorority under disguise as a chemistry tutor. Nevertheless we can't forget his head is made of peanut shells.

SORORITY GIRL CONFESSES

THREE PROMINENT GIRLS TELL HOW THEY DO IT

MEN ARE DEAD EASY IF YOU'RE ON TO THE GAME

It has been a question of much debate as to how some of the college coeds get by with their midnight campaigns in order to clear this question. Earnestine Biby, Edith Wilson and Wilma Roark have given a brief account of the way they do it.

It is best they say to choose a dark starless night when the wind is blowing. At twelve bells, take a dose of gruel which is composed of 20 per cent precaution 30 per cent civilianness and fifty per cent Coca Cola with aspirant tablets dissolved in it. At one o'clock they come out the kitchen door on low. That is how they get away from the house.

Then they love a little, fuss a little, and make up again and that is how they get away with the men. "Everything's dead easy even the men, if you know how to work them" said Edith. That's how we get away.

TO THE FACULTY

Here's to you old tops as good as you are
And to me as bad as I am
But as good as you are and as bad as I am
I'll as good as you are as bad as I am
—The Student

A fool there is (Woodhouse) who has made his prayer
To a rag and a bone and a hank of hair
We call her the wild woman who doesn't care
But the fool he calls her his Wilma fair
Not so with you and I

CO-EDS SEEK POPULARITY

COLLEGE WOMEN RACE MADLY INTO POLITICS.

THINK IT OVER GIRLS- IT'S ALL A MISTAKE

Some girls in this school have hitched their little red wagons to the moon beams of popularity and are working themselves thin to live up to their aspirations. Their idea of popularity is to hold as many offices on the hill as possible, be in all the beauty contests and have a hand on the reins of college politics in general.

Poor things! They carry tin buckets, wagon loads of college stationery have hollow eyes and sleepless nights. They rush madly from one committee meeting to the next. School pleasures are forfeited for a sham popularity which gets them no where, especially with the men.

They may see their names in print in every issue of the Collegian and their pictures are sprinkled here and there in great gobs through the College Annual but their names are not remembered in the hearts of the student body. There is a long string of stuff under their names when they graduate but what does that mean—Simply that they made a fool of themselves. They misinterpreted the phrase College Popularity.

Composition of a Sorority Girl

After a careful analysis, Professor West of the Chemistry department has submitted to our paper his results of a piece of research work as to the analysis of the modern sorority girl of today.

He announces that they are 30 per cent talking machine, 20 per cent vampire, 15 per cent nonsense, 10 per cent blank spots, 15 per cent snobbishness, 5 per cent beauty and 5 per cent loving.

The Grand Slam

"We"re Independent, We Are

Aquarium is Being Stocked

ANGLING IS SUCCESSFUL AT TIMES

Several Poor Fish Are Taken In.

Irregularly, intermittantly, and one at a time, specimens are being taken in to the Acquarium. Though not completely filled yet persistent fishing and the right kind of bait may land a sufficient nubmer to stock the place,

Last fall when the big rush was on only a few were nabbed and by now the choice prizes have been caught in the nets of other Greek anglers, or have been swallowed down stream by bigger fish.

The variety yet available seem to be unusually slippery and have been known to be almost landed when they flop back.

Those already in the acquarium are much alike. They have very little variety or anything, hard fins, brightly colored, rose and Nile green scales, and contentment with their lot. No doubt many of the other five sisterhoods have catches they would be glad to throw back if it were possible.

Next semester may bring a few victims in. Most of those who came in the fall school are too wary to nibble the hook. They are afraid of the lamp light or something.

Are The Quakers at K. S. A. C?

On a black midnight, in a raging thunderstorm, a Quaker came to the ford of a swollen stream. The thunder claps were deafening but the flashes were too brief to guide him across the torrent, se he knelt on the bank and prayed for a little less noise and a little more light.

Pax and Prix are cross at each other. The boys tried to run a candidate for assistant marshal and the girls simply wouldn't stand for it. Isn't it awful the way the men try to run things around this institution?

THE VET QUARTETTE

The veterinarians have a way
Of singing in the night
Indeed, its most pathetic
Is the Vet's musical plight.

Four nervy men stand in a row
And yell N'everything,
They put their heads together
And imagine they can sing.

Everyone in college.
Knows about the Vet quartette.
There's not a victim human
They've not serenaded yet.

Some time, some reckless member
Will try to baritone,
And the Vets will try their voices
On the ambulance telephone.

Kappa's Open House Success

The Kappas recently decided not to hold open house. It is rumored that the Betas felt slighted and took it upon remselves to see that one was given.

The fraternity of Beta Theta Pi had recently lost some of its valued property, namely, a stuffed owl that had been dead many years and was molting. As the owl holds a sacred place in the Kappa sorority they were blamed for its disappearance. Therefore when said owl disappeared the Betas took it upon themselves to visit the Kappas. They flocked into the hall and demanded their property but it was not forthcoming. No owl was in the possession of the Kappas as sufficient proof, and it is rumored that the Betas proceeded to hold open house. And still no owl could be found. Where, oh where is the Beta owl? Won't whoever took it, please return it?

Oliver Nelson was bitten by a mad dog last week but was immune from ill effects, being madder than the dog at the time he was nipped.

Fraternities Are Hit Hard

18th AMENDMENT RUSHES GREEKS TO K. C.

Barley Corn Family Had Friends In College.

It is with sincere regret that we have heard of the death of John Barleycorn. Our deepest sympathy goes out to the fraternities in their recent bereavement. Before his death the Sig Alpha and the Pi Kaps received daily telegrams concerning his health. When his condition became serious and there was little hope of his surviving, representatives were sent to offer their aid. It is rumored that the expenses of these representatives were paid and also financial aid was given to the Barleycorn family.

The fraternities supporting the family of John Barleycorn may find it impossible to keep up their own organizations and will probably call on the Betas for help. Should this be the case the Betas will probably be very glad to give financial aid to this cause.

The home of the Barleycorns has been in Missouri for the past ten years, but owing to their sudden bereavement they will spend seven years abroad. When they return they will probably spend their time at their home on Whiskey Island, three miles from the coast of New York.

John Barleycorn has been one of the prominent members of the Drinking Club in Kansas City, Missouri, for many years. He will be missed here probably more than anywhere else. The good old Irish Shamrocks will also miss him in their merrymaking for he was always one of their gayest members at their Irish wakes. The Sigma Phi Delts sent condolences by the quart. The Aztec did not hear of his death in time to take action. It is hoped that as Delta Tau's they will wake up. It is expected that the Sigma Nus will keep up their record in philanthropy and will not let this burden rest too heavily upon the

---

Push the K Out of K. U.

AGGIE FIVE OUT FOR GAME —ARE YOU?

Open Season On Jayhawk Killing.

The Kansas Aggies are playing their first title games this week. The Clevenger five will be remembered as having captured a title already apparently won from the Tigers in 1917.

In the smaller games played this winter the Aggies have displayed speed. Hinds, Bunger, Cowell and Jennings are fast, and Captain Clarke's dexterity in handling the ball rounds out a quintette which makes the opposing team bustle.

Inconsistency is the only trouble with the Aggie Team. In one game Bunger basketed a dozen goals and in the next only one. Coach Clevenger feels that they are tempermental.

K. U. always was our jinx. We never seem to have the right mascot when we go up against K. U. One might suggest a little pep as a mascot. Put the jinx on K. U.'s side and soak 'em next year in football. Now is the time to begin. Make K. U. rooters feel sick and weak, Give the "Rock Salt, Live Stock, Hey Rube" in the spirit of '76. Let's Go Aggies.

---

other organizations. Panhellenic may be able to apportion the amount correctly among them. In that case the Sig Eps should have a voice in the matter However, that is neither here nor there No single organization can decide a matter as weighty as that. Panhellenic must act as it thinks best. When the Delta Taus are admitted the balance of power will be restored

In Memoriam

Schlitz and Black Crow
And one clear quart for me
And may there be no moaning
At the bar from the fraternities
When I put out to sea

"Don't Bite the Hand That's Feeding You"

BEVERLY. KAN. *January 7* 1919   No. *97*
                                      83-667

THE UNION STATE BANK

PAY TO THE ORDER OF *Anne Marvelous Lorimer* $ *07/100*

Seven cents only ————————— DOLLARS

FOR *Meals to Date*   *John S. Painter*

A Grind's Saturday Night

Go hang yourself on a maplenut tree
And think you're a walnut Sundae,
For I've got to ram and jam and cram
To get my lessons by Monday.

✗ ✗ ✗ ✗

An "Aggie Girl's" Dad Expresses an Opinion

"Dear Daughter:
    No, I am not enclosing check. $75.00 a dozen is too much for the pictures you tell me about. They can not look like you and be worth that.
                                    Your loving Father."

✗ ✗ ✗ ✗

Senior—Did you answer that ring?
Freshman—I did.
Senior—What was it?
Freshman—It was somebody's alarm clock.

✗ ✗ ✗ ✗

The Motto that Kept Me Busy

You will miss something if you are not there.

DEAR PROFS

Odis Herschel

Hiram Herbert

Hallam Walker

Julius Ernest

Hallam Walk-ing

"Nancy"

Elden Valorius

Izit and Ducky

Florence

"Artie" and His Gang

You've All Heard About Dinner Work?

Song and dance of Miss D. S. Lettus —
entitled "Safely Through Another Salade".

Dinner Work is a "nothing to be scared over" that meets home economics girls at the train their freshman year and hangs oppressively heavy on them until it flattens them out their senior year. It is traditional that such girls lie awake the entire night before they serve an informal luncheon to four ordinary persons. If they pull a bone, such as stepping to the left side instead of the right, they are ashamed to go through main hall until they have forgotten their disgrace.

They only have so much money to spend on their meals and for this reason have sprung up little economies that make your heart ache. Way back at the beginning some enterprising woman saved money on lettuce and they have been doing it ever since. Lettuce leaves that at the end of the meal came out from under the salad unharmed, uneaten, decorated another person's salad the next day. The other girls copied this cleverness and soon the great outside heard about it, and senior men, either desiring to be popular with the cook, or else fearing the lettuce leaf's past, protected each green leaf as though it were a part of his life. A nickel's worth of lettuce thus could be used a week and then chopped up and eaten the last day.

This practice was traditional even in 1912. It might have gone on forever, but this year conscientious Vera asked her horror stricken critic what would happen if someone should eat theirs. The horror stricken teacher said indignantly that this was the first time such a hideous economy had been practiced, which of course made everybody laugh. D. S. instructors with snappish eyes asked each other how long this had been going on, and when they found out they just hushed up and put an awful stop to the all-week stands of the faithful lettuce leaf.

Page 355

Jacob Reed's Sons

MANUFACTURERS OF

UNIFORMS *of* QUALITY

For leading Military Colleges and Schools throughout the United States

The Uniforms worn by students of the Kansas State Agricultural College are finished examples of the quality and appearance of our product

JACOB REED'S SONS

1424-1426 CHESTNUT STREET

PHILADELPHIA

It was bad enough to have Sara Chase Yost, but what about the way Nadia Dunn Corby?

⊠ ⊠ ⊠ ⊠

Weren't we surprised, though, that day we came back to school at noon and found out that the May Queen had been elected. It was all done, too, while we drank soda water at Jonnie's.

Jokes of professors oft remind us,
We can make our grades sublime
If we will only burst with laughter
At the designated time.

He asked her: "Will you marry me?"
In quite the usual way.
She answered: "No, sir; I will NOT,"
But he spelt it with a "K"

Be careful, friend Ike,
When you're on a hike
That you don't pull off a "Bone."
For the seas will be foamin'
And your boat will be roamin'
If you lose the chaperone.

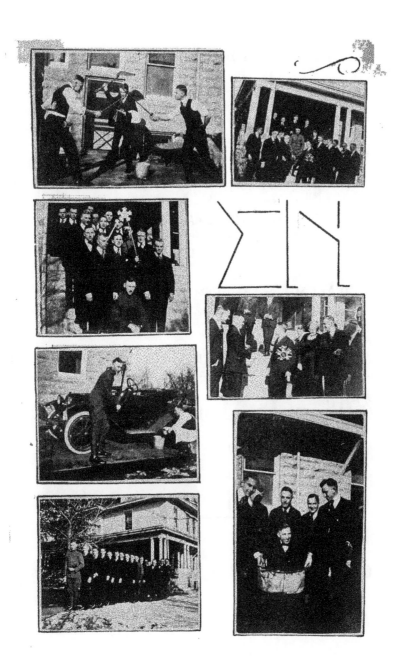

John Deere Plow Company
Kansas City, Missouri

The Largest Implement House in the World

John Deere Farm Implements, Vehicles and Farm Wagons

Page 361

How to Graduate With Honors

1. Spend Saturday evening studying.
2. Contest every grade below "E."
3. Yell "you're a liar" when you know that the prof is feeding you.
4. Proclaim in public that you consider water unsanitary for the purpose of cleansing the body.
5. Tip the motorman on every ride to the city.
6. Read every reference they tell you to.
7. Bring suit against all profs who realize how little you know.
8. Refuse to have your hair cut, shoes shined or chin shaved until after you have made Phi Kappa Phi.

GILLETT HOTEL

BOONE & POLAND, PROPRIETORS

A Refined Hotel for Your Mother, Wife and Sister

UNEQUALED FACILITIES FOR SERVING LARGE AND SMALL BANQUETS

Sunday Evening Suppers a Specialty

Maybe This Happened to Amy Lowell

I laid my empty head
Above where I judged his heart was
and waited—
For rainbow-colored thrills—
But I stuck my ear
On the fountain pen
He writes his checks with.

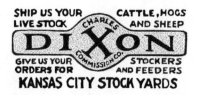

Society Brand Clothes

and You College Men

MAKE THE

KNOSTMAN STORE

WHAT IT IS TODAY

The Greatest Outfitters to Men and Young Men

PALACE
D R U G
COMPANY

TWO STORES
115 South Fourth Street
1226 Moro Street

Kodaks and Supplies

K. S. A. C. also
Has its dear traditions.
One of them is
To go to chapel and sit
On the rim.
Another is to search for pep.
Sometimes a little
Is stirred up,
Then someone in a low voice
Comes by and sends the
Gang home.
Persons taking what they call
Zoo
Discuss it freely and
Get hard boiled about
Cats.
The men rent dress suits
But wear their own
Yellow shoes.
Girls try to keep each other
From getting to
Their own mail
Boxes. They stand
And lean against them if
Necessary. There are other
Traditions also besides these.

FAIRBANKS--1
SCALES

Fairbanks - Morse
Oil Engines
Electric Lighting Plants
Power Pumping Plants
Hay Presses

FAIRBANKS
Morse & Co.
Kansas City, Mo.

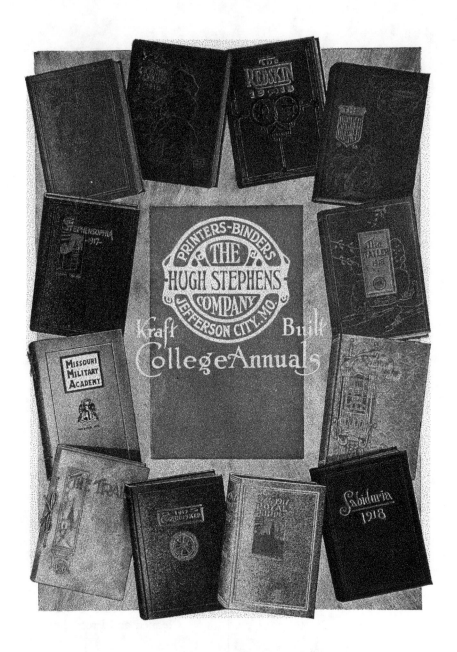

This Annual Printed and Bound by

THE HUGH STEPHENS PRINTING CO.
JEFFERSON CITY, MO.

The largest, most uniquely equipped modern plant in the west, specializing in the design and production of "Kraft Built College Annuals."

Our Service Department will render expert assistance without charge and supply complete blank forms dealing with the latest method of Advertising Campaigns and Editorial Systems for College Annuals.

Helpful advice and ideas given on art work for Opening Pages and Division Sheets, View Sections and Beauty Sections, combining Kraft-like bindings, papers and inks into beautiful artistic books—SUCCESSFULLY FINANCED.

Write for estimates and samples.

A COLLEGE ANNUAL, designed, planned and engraved by Burger Engraving Company, always results in a successful publication. ¶ College Annual Staffs have discovered that our close co-operation, combined with original and snappy ideas, the highest quality of engraving and service, result in a financial statement that shows a profit to the Staff. ¶ May we talk over our proposition with you?

Burger
Engraving Co.
Eighth and Wyandotte : Kansas City

Hotel Muehlebach

Baltimore Avenue and Twelfth Street
Kansas City, Mo.

Utility ~ Service ~ Elegance
Opened in May 1915

Ultra-modern in equipment,
complete washed air ventilating system

Unique in the courtesy of its
Service

500 Rooms   Rate from $2.00

Operated by
Whitmore Hotel Company
Under the Personal Direction of
S.J. Whitmore and Joseph Reichl

Bold, Bad Man

Where's That Ten-spot

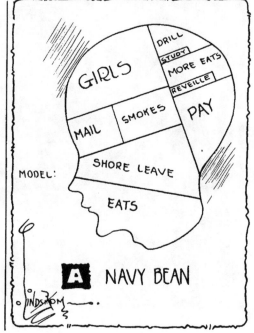

It's a pleasure to bake with

For it represents the final word in quality.
Its wonderful goodness never varies.

The H. D. Lee Flour Mills Company
Salina, Kansas

THE MANHATTAN NATIONALIST

Daily and Weekly   *Fine Job and Book Work*

Special attention given to students and college printing.

No matter where you find us we boost for K. S. A. C.

GUEST'S STORE

CLAY CENTER, KANSAS

GUEST'S STORE is in business first to serve the public. And service is the keynote of its success. It gives good service by having a well equipped stock of the best quality. Customers are assured of courteous treatment and sincere sales. Every effort is made to give the person who buys of Guest's exactly what he wants.

Guest's are running their store to accommodate your tastes and desires.

THE STORE THAT SERVES

JUST ONE WORD MORE—

If,
You are irritated
By names spelled incorrectly—
Just stop and think, a minute.
If you helped on
The Royal Purple
It was probably
You
Who mis-spelled them.
And, if you didn't
Help any
In this year of
Flu epidemics
and high prices,
and war conditions,
and uncertainties,
and no money,
and late start,
Well—
Surely you haven't the nerve to kick!

Thanks,
Everybody—
And if you hear
of a job
Any place,
Tell the boss
That
We have had
EXPERIENCE.

CPSIA information can be obtained
at www.ICGtesting.com
Printed in the USA
BVHW060114061118
532208BV00018B/2037/P